Wonderful ways to prepare

STEWS & CASSEROLES

by JO ANN SHIRLEY

OTHER TITLES IN THIS SERIES

1. HORS D'ŒUVRES & FIRST COURSES

2. SOUPS

3. MEAT

4. FISH & SEAFOOD

5. STEWS & CASSEROLES

6. SALADS

7. DESSERTS

8. CAKES & COOKIES

9. BARBECUES

10. ITALIAN FOOD

Printed in Canada.

Wonderful ways to prepare
STEWS & CASSEROLES

PLAYMORE INC NEW YORK USA
UNDER ARRANGEMENT WITH
I. WALDMAN & SON INC

AYERS & JAMES PTY LTD
CROWS NEST AUSTRALIA

STAFFORD PEMBERTON PUBLISHING
KNUTSFORD UNITED KINGDOM

FIRST PUBLISHED 1978

PUBLISHED IN THE USA
BY PLAYMORE INC.
UNDER ARRANGEMENT WITH I. WALDMAN & SON INC.

PUBLISHED IN AUSTRALIA
BY AYERS & JAMES PTY. LTD.
CROWS NEST.   AUSTRALIA

PUBLISHED IN THE UNITED KINGDOM
BY STAFFORD PEMBERTON PUBLISHING
KNUTSFORD CHESIRE

ISBN 0 86908 058 X

OVEN TEMPERATURE GUIDE

Description	Gas		Electric		Mark
	C	F	C	F	
Cool	100	200	110	225	¼
Very Slow	120	250	120	250	½
Slow	150	300	150	300	1-2
Moderately slow	160	325	170	340	3
Moderate	180	350	200	400	4
Moderately hot	190	375	220	425	5-6
Hot	200	400	230	450	6-7
Very hot	230	450	250	475	8-9

LIQUID MEASURES

IMPERIAL	METRIC
1 teaspoon	5 ml
1 tablespoon	20 ml
2 fluid ounces (¼ cup)	62.5 ml
4 fluid ounces (½ cup)	125 ml
8 fluid ounces (1 cup)	250 ml
1 pint (16 ounces — 2 cups)*	500 ml

* (The imperial pint is equal to 20 fluid ounces.)

SOLID MEASURES

AVOIRDUPOIS	METRIC
1 ounce	30 g
4 ounces (¼ lb)	125 g
8 ounces (½ lb)	250 g
12 ounces (¾ lb)	375 g
16 ounces (1 lb)	500 g
24 ounces (1½ lb)	750 g
32 ounces (2 lb)	1000 g (1 kg)

CUP AND SPOON REPLACEMENTS FOR OUNCES

INGREDIENT	½ oz	1 oz	2 oz	3 oz	4 oz	5 oz	6 oz	7 oz	8 oz
Almonds, ground	2 T	¼ C	½ C	¾ C	1¼ C	1⅓ C	1⅔ C	2 C	2¼ C
slivered	6 t	¼ C	½ C	¾ C	1 C	1⅓ C	1⅔ C	2 C	2¼ C
whole	2 T	¼ C	⅓ C	½ C	¾ C	1 C	1¼ C	1⅓ C	1½ C
Apples, dried whole	3 T	½ C	1 C	1⅓ C	2 C	2⅓ C	2¾ C	3⅓ C	3¾ C
Apricots, chopped	2 T	¼ C	½ C	¾ C	1 C	1¼ C	1½ C	1¾ C	2 C
whole	2 T	3 T	½ C	⅔ C	1 C	1¼ C	1⅓ C	1½ C	1¾ C
Arrowroot	1 T	2 T	⅓ C	½ C	⅔ C	¾ C	1 C	1¼ C	1⅓ C
Baking Powder	1 T	2 T	⅓ C	½ C	⅔ C	¾ C	1 C	1 C	1¼ C
Baking Soda	1 T	2 T	⅓ C	½ C	⅔ C	¾ C	1 C	1 C	1¼ C
Barley	1 T	2 T	¼ C	½ C	⅔ C	¾ C	1 C	1 C	1¼ C
Breadcrumbs, dry	2 T	¼ C	½ C	¾ C	1 C	1¼ C	1½ C	1¾ C	2 C
soft	¼ C	½ C	1 C	1½ C	2 C	2½ C	3 C	3⅔ C	4¼ C
Biscuit Crumbs	2 T	¼ C	½ C	¾ C	1¼ C	1⅓ C	1⅔ C	2 C	2¼ C
Butter	3 t	6 t	¼ C	⅓ C	½ C	⅔ C	¾ C	1 C	1 C
Cheese, grated, lightly packed,									
natural cheddar	6 t	¼ C	½ C	¾ C	1 C	1¼ C	1½ C	1¾ C	2 C
Processed cheddar	5 t	2 T	⅓ C	⅔ C	¾ C	1 C	1¼ C	1½ C	1⅔ C
Parmesan, Romano	6 t	¼ C	½ C	¾ C	1 C	1⅓ C	1⅔ C	2 C	2¼ C
Cherries, candied, chopped	1 T	2 T	⅓ C	½ C	¾ C	1 C	1 C	1⅓ C	1½ C
whole	1 T	2 T	⅓ C	½ C	⅔ C	¾ C	1 C	1¼ C	1⅓ C
Cocoa	2 T	¼ C	½ C	¾ C	1¼ C	1⅓ C	1⅔ C	2 C	2¼ C
Coconut, desiccated	2 T	⅓ C	⅔ C	1 C	1⅓ C	1⅔ C	2 C	2⅓ C	2⅔ C
shredded	⅓ C	⅔ C	1¼ C	1¾ C	2½ C	3 C	3⅔ C	4⅓ C	5 C
Cornstarch	6 t	3 T	½ C	⅔ C	1 C	1¼ C	1½ C	1⅔ C	2 C
Corn Syrup	2 t	1 T	2 T	¼ C	⅓ C	½ C	½ C	⅔ C	⅔ C
Coffee, ground	2 T	⅓ C	⅔ C	1 C	1⅓ C	1⅔ C	2 C	2⅓ C	2⅔ C
instant	3 T	½ C	1 C	1⅓ C	1¾ C	2¼ C	2⅔ C	3 C	3½ C
Cornflakes	½ C	1 C	2 C	3 C	4¼ C	5¼ C	6¼ C	7⅓ C	8⅓ C
Cream of Tartar	1 T	2 T	⅓ C	½ C	⅔ C	¾ C	1 C	1 C	1¼ C
Currants	1 T	2 T	⅓ C	⅔ C	¾ C	1 C	1¼ C	1½ C	1⅔ C
Custard Powder	6 t	3 T	½ C	⅔ C	1 C	1¼ C	1½ C	1⅔ C	2 C
Dates, chopped	1 T	2 T	⅓ C	⅔ C	¾ C	1 C	1¼ C	1½ C	1⅔ C
whole, pitted	1 T	2 T	⅓ C	½ C	¾ C	1 C	1¼ C	1⅓ C	1½ C
Figs, chopped	1 T	2 T	⅓ C	½ C	¾ C	1 C	1 C	1⅓ C	1½ C
Flour, all-purpose or cake	6 t	¼ C	½ C	¾ C	1 C	1¼ C	1½ C	1¾ C	2 C
wholemeal	6 t	3 T	½ C	⅔ C	1 C	1¼ C	1⅓ C	1⅔ C	1¾ C
Fruit, mixed	1 T	2 T	⅓ C	½ C	¾ C	1 C	1¼ C	1⅓ C	1½ C
Gelatine	5 t	2 T	⅓ C	½ C	¾ C	1 C	1 C	1¼ C	1½ C
Ginger, crystallised pieces	1 T	2 T	⅓ C	½ C	¾ C	1 C	1¼ C	1⅓ C	1½ C
ground	6 t	⅓ C	½ C	¾ C	1¼ C	1½ C	1¾ C	2 C	2¼ C
preserved, heavy syrup	1 T	2 T	⅓ C	½ C	⅔ C	¾ C	1 C	1 C	1¼ C
Glucose, liquid	2 t	1 T	2 T	¼ C	⅓ C	½ C	½ C	⅔ C	⅔ C
Haricot Beans	1 T	2 T	⅓ C	½ C	⅔ C	¾ C	1 C	1 C	1¼ C

In this table, t represents teaspoonful, T represents tablespoonful and C represents cupful.

CUP AND SPOON REPLACEMENTS FOR OUNCES (Cont.)

INGREDIENT	½ oz	1 oz	2 oz	3 oz	4 oz	5 oz	6 oz	7 oz	8 oz
Honey	2 t	1 T	2 T	¼ C	⅓ C	½ C	½ C	⅔ C	⅔ C
Jam	2 t	1 T	2 T	¼ C	⅓ C	½ C	½ C	⅔ C	¾ C
Lentils	1 T	2 T	⅓ C	½ C	⅔ C	¾ C	1 C	1 C	1¼ C
Macaroni (see pasta)									
Milk Powder, full cream	2 T	¼ C	½ C	¾ C	1¼ C	1⅓ C	1⅔ C	2 C	2¼ C
non fat	2 T	⅓ C	¾ C	1¼ C	1½ C	2 C	2⅓ C	2¾ C	3¼ C
Nutmeg	6 t	3 T	½ C	⅔ C	¾ C	1 C	1¼ C	1½ C	1⅔ C
Nuts, chopped	6 t	¼ C	½ C	¾ C	1 C	1¼ C	1½ C	1¾ C	2 C
Oatmeal	1 T	2 T	½ C	⅔ C	¾ C	1 C	1¼ C	1½ C	1⅔ C
Olives, whole	1 T	2 T	⅓ C	⅔ C	¾ C	1 C	1¼ C	1½ C	1⅔ C
sliced	1 T	2 T	⅓ C	⅔ C	¾ C	1 C	1¼ C	1½ C	1⅔ C
Pasta, short (e.g. macaroni)	1 T	2 T	⅓ C	⅔ C	¾ C	1 C	1¼ C	1½ C	1⅔ C
Peaches, dried & whole	1 T	2 T	⅓ C	⅔ C	¾ C	1 C	1¼ C	1½ C	1⅔ C
chopped	6 t	¼ C	½ C	¾ C	1 C	1¼ C	1½ C	1¾ C	2 C
Peanuts, shelled, raw, whole	1 T	2 T	⅓ C	½ C	¾ C	1 C	1¼ C	1⅓ C	1½ C
roasted	1 T	2 T	⅓ C	⅔ C	¾ C	1 C	1¼ C	1½ C	1⅔ C
Peanut Butter	3 t	6 t	3 T	⅓ C	½ C	½ C	⅔ C	¾ C	1 C
Peas, split	1 T	2 T	⅓ C	½ C	⅔ C	¾ C	1 C	1 C	1¼ C
Peel, mixed	1 T	2 T	⅓ C	½ C	¾ C	1 C	1 C	1¼ C	1½ C
Potato, powder	1 T	2 T	¼ C	⅓ C	½ C	⅔ C	¾ C	1 C	1¼ C
flakes	¼ C	½ C	1 C	1⅓ C	2 C	2⅓ C	2¾ C	3⅓ C	3¾ C
Prunes, chopped	1 T	2 T	⅓ C	½ C	⅔ C	¾ C	1 C	1¼ C	1⅓ C
whole pitted	1 T	2 T	⅓ C	½ C	⅔ C	¾ C	1 C	1 C	1¼ C
Raisins	2 T	¼ C	⅓ C	½ C	¾ C	1 C	1 C	1⅓ C	1½ C
Rice, short grain, raw	1 T	2 T	¼ C	½ C	⅔ C	¾ C	1 C	1 C	1¼ C
long grain, raw	1 T	2 T	⅓ C	½ C	¾ C	1 C	1¼ C	1⅓ C	1½ C
Rice Bubbles	⅔ C	1¼ C	2½ C	3⅔ C	5 C	6¼ C	7½ C	8¾ C	10 C
Rolled Oats	2 T	⅓ C	⅔ C	1 C	1⅓ C	1¾ C	2 C	2½ C	2¾ C
Sago	2 T	¼ C	⅓ C	½ C	¾ C	1 C	1 C	1¼ C	1½ C
Salt, common	3 t	6 t	¼ C	⅓ C	½ C	⅔ C	¾ C	1 C	1 C
Semolina	1 T	2 T	⅓ C	½ C	¾ C	1 C	1 C	1⅓ C	1½ C
Spices	6 t	3 T	¼ C	⅓ C	½ C	½ C	⅔ C	¾ C	1 C
Sugar, plain	3 t	6 t	¼ C	⅓ C	½ C	⅔ C	¾ C	1 C	1 C
confectioners'	1 T	2 T	⅓ C	½ C	¾ C	1 C	1 C	1¼ C	1½ C
moist brown	1 T	2 T	⅓ C	½ C	¾ C	1 C	1 C	1⅓ C	1½ C
Tapioca	1 T	2 T	⅓ C	½ C	⅔ C	¾ C	1 C	1¼ C	1⅓ C
Treacle	2 t	1 T	2 T	¼ C	⅓ C	½ C	½ C	⅔ C	⅔ C
Walnuts, chopped	2 T	¼ C	½ C	¾ C	1 C	1¼ C	1½ C	1¾ C	2 C
halved	2 T	⅓ C	⅔ C	1 C	1¼ C	1½ C	1¾ C	2¼ C	2½ C
Yeast, dried	6 t	3 T	½ C	⅔ C	1 C	1¼ C	1⅓ C	1⅔ C	1¾ C
compressed	3 t	6 t	3 T	⅓ C	½ C	½ C	⅔ C	¾ C	1 C

In this table, t represents teaspoonful, T represents tablespoonful and C represents cupful.

Contents

Beef... 9
Chicken 41
Lamb 50
Fish & Seafoods 64
Pork & Ham 74
Others 89

Beef

Beef and Potato Casserole

2 lb (1 kg) potatoes
½ cup (125 g) butter or margarine
½ cup (125 ml) cream
1 egg, beaten
¼ teaspoon nutmeg
3 teaspoons salt

3 onions, chopped
2 lb (1 kg) stewing beef, cut into ½ inch (1 cm) cubes
½ cup (125 ml) beef stock
½ teaspoon black pepper
1 bay leaf
¼ cup dry breadcrumbs

1. Cook the unpeeled potatoes until tender. Drain, peel and mash. Beat in 3 tablespoons (60 g) butter or margarine, the cream, egg, nutmeg and 1½ teaspoons salt until very light and fluffy.
2. Melt the remaining butter or margarine in a large saucepan. Saute the onions for five minutes.
3. Add the meat and cook over a high heat, stirring constantly, until the meat is browned. Mix in the stock, pepper, bay leaf and remaining salt. Cook over a low heat for twenty minutes. Discard the bay leaf.
4. In a greased casserole, arrange as many layers as possible the potatoes and meat mixture, starting and ending with the potatoes.
5. Sprinkle with the bread crumbs and dot with a little butter. Bake in a 400°F (200°C) oven for twenty-five minutes or until browned.

Serves 6-8.

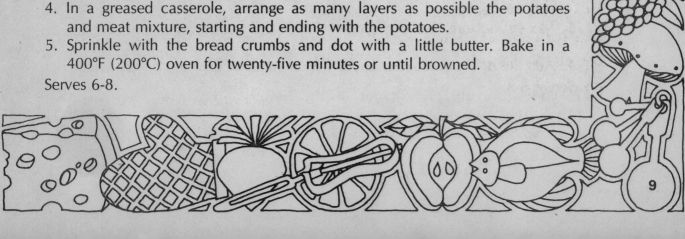

Beef Stew Toulouse

3 tablespoons (60 g) butter or margarine	1 cup (210 g) uncooked rice
3 lb (1½ kg) rump steak, cut into ½ inch (1 cm) cubes	1 can corn niblets, drained
2 onions, sliced	1 cup finely sliced green peppers
2 tomatoes, peeled and sliced	¼ teaspoon saffron
2 teaspoons salt	2 teaspoons brown sugar
¼ teaspoon freshly ground black pepper	1 cup (250 ml) dry white wine
	1 cup (250 ml) beef stock
	⅛ teaspoon cinnamon

1. Melt the butter or margarine in a large saucepan. Brown the meat in it.
2. Add the onions, tomatoes, salt and pepper. Cover and cook over medium heat for ten minutes.
3. Mix in the rice, corn, green pepper, saffron, sugar, wine, stock and cinnamon. Cover and cook over a low heat for 20 minutes or until the rice is tender.

Serves 6-8.

West Indian Beef Stew

3 lb (1½ kg) chuck steak, cut in one-inch (2 cm) cubes	1 clove garlic, crushed
½ cup flour	1 lb (500 g) tomatoes, peeled and quartered
2 teaspoons salt	1 teaspoon powdered ginger
½ teaspoon pepper	2 cups (420 g) half-cooked rice
⅓ cup (83 ml) oil	
1 large onion, chopped	

1. Toss the beef in a mixture of the flour, salt and pepper. Heat the oil in a large saucepan and brown the meat in it very well. Pour off the fat.
2. Add the onion and garlic and cook until the onion begins to brown, stirring frequently.
3. Mix in the tomatoes and ginger. Cover and cook over a low heat for 2 hours.
4. Add the rice and cook for another 20 minutes or until the rice is tender.

Serves 6-8.

Beans and Beef

2 cups dried beans (your choice)
3 tablespoons oil
3 lb (1½ kg) chuck steak, cut
   into bite-size pieces
2 onions, chopped

2 tablespoons honey
2 teaspoons salt
½ teaspoon pepper
1½ teaspoons prepared mustard

1. Soak the beans in enough water to cover overnight. Simmer the beans in the water in which they soaked for about 20 minutes. Drain the beans reserving the water.
2. Heat the oil in a large saucepan and saute the onions.
3. Add the meat and cook until the meat is browned.
4. Mix the honey, salt, pepper and mustard with the reserved bean water. (Add more water if necessary to make 3 cups.)
5. Add the beans to the meat. Mix well. Stir in the liquid, cover and simmer for about 3 hours or until meat is tender.

Serves 8.

Ground Beef and Macaroni Casserole

1 cup (150 g) macaroni
2 onions, chopped
4 stalks celery, sliced
1 red pepper, chopped
2½ tablespoons (50 g) butter
   or margarine
1 lb (500 g) ground beef

1 can (445 g) condensed
   mushroom soup
1 can water
salt and pepper
½ teaspoon marjoram
2 tablespoons chopped parsley

1. Cook the macaroni in salted boiling water until just tender.
2. Saute the onions, celery and pepper in the butter or margarine for about five minutes. Add the meat and cook for another five minutes.
3. Mix in the soup, water, salt and pepper to taste, marjoram and parsley.
4. Put the cooked macaroni in the bottom of a greased casserole dish. Cover with meat mixture. Cover and cook in a 350°F (180°C) oven for about one hour.

Serves 4.

Ground Beef and Celery Casserole

½ bunch celery, sliced
1 onion, chopped
2 tablespoons (40 g) butter
  or margarine
salt and pepper
4 tablespoons flour
1 lb (500 g) ground beef

4 tomatoes, sliced
1¼ cups (300 ml) beef stock
Biscuit topping:
1 cup flour
2½ tablespoons (50 g) butter
  or margarine
milk

1. Saute the celery and onion in the butter or margarine. Put into a casserole dish.
2. Season and flour the meat and brown it in the butter. Add to the casserole with the tomatoes and stock. Cover and cook in a 350°F (180°C) oven for 45 minutes.
3. While the meat is cooking, make the biscuit topping by mixing the flour with the butter or margarine and adding enough milk to make a soft dough. Roll out to a thickness of ½ inch (1 cm). Cut into rounds and put on top of the casserole. Glaze with milk.
4. Cook the casserole with the biscuit topping uncovered for about 15 minutes.

Serves 4-6.

Shin of Beef and Vegetable Casserole

2 lb (1 kg) shin of beef
2 tablespoons oil
2 tablespoons flour
1 teaspoon dry mustard
1½ teaspoons salt
1½ tablespoons brown sugar
2½ cups (625 ml) tomato juice

salt and pepper
½ cauliflower, cut in flowerets
1 carrot, diced
1 onion, sliced
1 cup chopped celery
1 green pepper, chopped

1. In a frypan heat the oil and brown the meat. Remove to a casserole dish.
2. Mix the flour, mustard, salt and brown sugar in the frypan with the remaining oil. Slowly add the tomato juice, stirring constantly. Pour over the meat. Cover and cook for two hours in a 325°F (160°C) oven.
3. Remove bones and cut meat into bite-size pieces. Add vegetables and cook for another 45 minutes or until the vegetables are tender.

Serves 6.

Pepper Pot Stew

2 lb (1 kg) lean stewing beef	1 cup sliced carrots
¼ cup flour	1 large potato, diced
2 tablespoons oil	1 onion, chopped
3 cups (750 ml) beef stock	½ teaspoon black pepper
1½ teaspoons salt	2 tablespoons parsley, chopped

1. Cut beef into one-inch (2½ cm) cubes. Cover meat with flour and brown on all sides in hot oil in a large saucepan.
2. Add salt and stock and cook, covered, for about 2 hours or until meat is tender.
3. Add vegetables, pepper and parsley and cook until vegetables are tender.

Serves 6.

Rump Steak and Olive Casserole

1 lb (500 g) rump steak	1 clove garlic, crushed
3 tablespoons oil	4 peppercorns
1 carrot, sliced	salt and pepper
2 small onions, sliced	¾ lb (375 g) bacon
3 stalks celery, sliced	¼ lb (125 g) black olives, halved
1¼ cup (300 ml) red wine	and pitted
½ cup (125 ml) wine vinegar	4 tomatoes
2 tablespoons chopped parsley	

1. Heat the oil in a saucepan. Saute the carrot, onions and celery for ten minutes. Add half the red wine, all the vinegar, parsley, garlic, peppercorns and salt and pepper to taste. Bring to a boil, reduce heat and simmer for 15 minutes. Cool.
2. Cut the meat into cubes and cover with strained marinade. Allow to stand for about one hour.
3. Fry the bacon until crispy. Remove the bacon and brown the drained steak. Put into a casserole dish. Add the marinade to the meat with the bacon, wine and olives.
4. Cover and cook in a 325°F (160°C) oven for about two hours. Add sliced tomatoes for the last 15 minutes of cooking.

Serves 4.

Fruity Hotpot

1½ lb (750 g) braising steak, cut up
2 onions, sliced
3 cooking apples, peeled, cored and sliced
3 tomatoes, sliced
1 tablespoon oil
curry powder to taste

⅓ cup (60 g) currants
⅓ cup (55 g) raisins
1½ cups (375 ml) beef stock
1½ tablespoons flour
salt
1 tablespoon brown sugar
3 hard-boiled eggs
2 tablespoons chopped parsley

1. Heat the oil in a large saucepan. Lightly fry the meat, onions and apples until golden brown. Add the tomatoes and curry powder to taste and cook for a further five minutes.
2. Place the mixture in a casserole dish. Stir in the currants and raisins. Cover and cook in a 350°F (180°C) oven for 2 hours.
3. Blend the flour with a little water. Stir into the casserole. Season to taste with salt. Add brown sugar.
4. Garnish with slices of egg and chopped parsley.

Serves 6.

Beef Stroganoff

2 tablespoons (40 g) butter or margarine
3 lb (1½ kg) rump steak, cut into thin strips
3 large onions
½ lb (250 g) fresh mushrooms
2 bay leaves

1 teaspoon salt
⅛ teaspoon pepper
1 teaspoon Worcestershire sauce
½ cup (125 ml) water
1 cup (250 ml) sherry
2 cups (500 g) sour cream

1. Melt the butter or margarine in a dutch oven or fire-proof casserole dish. Add meat and onions and saute until meat is brown and onions golden brown.
2. Add mushrooms, bay leaves, salt, pepper, water and Worcestershire sauce. Bring to a boil. Reduce heat, cover and cook slowly for one hour. Remove from heat and cool.
3. Gradually add sherry. Reheat and cook for another half hour. Cool again.
4. When ready to serve add sour cream and reheat but do not boil.

Serves 6.

Leftover Beef Casserole

2 cups chopped cooked beef
2 medium onions, sliced
1 tablespoon (20 g) butter
   or margarine
2 cups sliced cooked carrots
1 teaspoon salt
¼ teaspoon pepper

4 medium potatoes,
   cooked and mashed
½ cup (125 ml) cream
1 teaspoon Worcestershire sauce
4 tablespoons dry bread crumbs
1 tablespoon (20 g) butter or
   margarine, melted

1. Melt the butter or margarine in a frypan and saute the onions until golden brown.
2. Put the onions on the bottom of a casserole dish. Add a layer of chopped beef and a layer of carrots. Continue layering until the beef and carrots are all used. Season with salt and pepper after each layer.
3. Cover with mashed potatoes.
4. Mix cream with Worcestershire sauce and pour over the potatoes.
5. Mix bread crumbs with melted butter or margarine. Sprinkle on top of casserole.
6. Cook uncovered in a 400°F (200°C) oven until browned and heated through.

Serves 6.

Chili Con Carne

2 lb (1 kg) boneless beef,
   ground or cut into small cubes
3 tablespoons vegetable oil
3 onions, thinly sliced
1 green pepper, chopped
1 lb (500 g) tomatoes, chopped

2 teaspoons salt
½ teaspoon black pepper
chili powder to taste
2 cloves garlic, crushed
1 lb (500 g) canned kidney beans

1. Heat the oil in a saucepan. Saute the onions and green pepper for ten minutes.
2. Add the meat and cook over a medium heat, stirring constantly, until browned.
3. Mix in the tomatoes, salt, pepper, chili powder and garlic. Cover and cook over a low heat for 1½ hours. Add a little water if necessary.
4. Add the beans, taste for seasoning and cook for 15 minutes longer.

Serves 4-6.

Family Meat Pie

2 lb (1 kg) ground beef	1 cup cooked peas
1 tablespoon butter or margarine	½ cup sliced celery
1 beef stock cube	salt
1½ cups (375 ml) hot tomato juice	1 egg, separated
1 cup cooked carrots, sliced	3 cups hot mashed potatoes

1. Season meat with salt and brown in the butter or margarine, stirring occasionally, until the meat browns.
2. Dissolve the stock cube in the tomato juice and add to the meat. Cook for 5-8 minutes. Remove from heat.
3. Add the cooked vegetables to the meat and season to taste with salt.
4. Beat the egg yolk and add to the mashed potatoes. Fold in the stiffly beaten egg white. Spread the bottom of a baking dish with half of the mashed potatoes. Add the meat and vegetable mixture and top with remaining mashed potatoes.
5. Bake in a 400°F (200°C) oven for fifteen minutes.

Serves 6.

Braised Liver Casserole

1 lb (500 g) beef or lamb liver	1 red pepper, chopped
¼ cup flour	2 potatoes, sliced
1½ teaspoons salt	1 cup (250 ml) beef stock
¼ teaspoon pepper	½ lb (250 g) tomatoes,
2 tablespoons oil	chopped
2 carrots, cubed	1 bay leaf
1 onion, sliced	

1. Cut liver into two-inch (5 cm) squares. Roll in flour which has been seasoned with salt and pepper. Brown in hot oil.
2. Remove liver and brown carrots, onion, pepper and potatoes. Remove vegetables and blend in any remaining flour left from dredging liver. Stir in beef stock and tomatoes.
3. Combine gravy with liver and vegetables. Add bay leaf and pour into casserole dish. Cover.
4. Bake in a 350°F (180°C) oven for one hour.

Serves 4.

Leftover Beef Stew

2 tablespoons (40 g) butter or margarine
2 tablespoons flour
2 cups (500 ml) dry red wine
1 teaspoon salt
½ teaspoon black pepper
2 tomatoes, peeled and chopped
3 white onions, quartered
6 potatoes, peeled and quartered
2 tablespoons chopped parsley
¼ teaspoon thyme
1 bay leaf
4 cups cooked beef, cut into small cubes
½ lb (250 g) green beans, cut in one-inch (2½ cm) pieces

1. Melt the butter or margarine in a saucepan. Blend in the flour until browned. Gradually add the wine, stirring constantly, until at the boiling point.
2. Add the salt and pepper, tomatoes, onions, potatoes, parsley, thyme and bay leaf. Cook over a low heat for 45 minutes.
3. Add the beef and the beans and cook for 15 minutes longer. Discard the bay leaf.

Serves 6.

Red Cabbage and Beef Stew

2 tablespoons oil
3 lb (1½ kg) chuck steak, cut into one-inch (2½ cm) cubes
2 onions, thinly sliced
2 teaspoons salt
½ teaspoon black pepper
1 teaspoon caraway seeds
2 cups (500 ml) boiling water
¼ cup (62.5 ml) vinegar
4 tablespoons brown sugar
4 cups coarsely shredded red cabbage
1 teaspoon powdered ginger

1. Heat the oil in a saucepan and brown the meat and onions in it. Add the salt, pepper, caraway seeds and water. Cover and cook over a low heat for one hour.
2. Mix in the vinegar, sugar, cabbage, ginger and a little more water if necessary. Recover and cook for another hour or until meat is tender.

Serves 6-8.

Beef with Eggplant Casserole

2 lb (1 kg) fillet of beef
1 medium eggplant
¼ cup flour
⅓ cup (83 ml) oil
4 medium tomatoes, chopped
1 clove garlic, crushed

2 teaspoons salt
½ teaspoon black pepper
¼ teaspoon basil
3 tablespoons chopped parsley
¼ cup dry bread crumbs

1. Cut the beef into ¼-inch (½ cm) thick slices.
2. Peel the eggplant and slice ¼-inch (½ cm) thick. Dip the eggplant in the flour. Heat ¼ cup (62.5 ml) of the oil in a frypan. Brown the eggplant in it.
3. Arrange the eggplant on the bottom of a greased casserole dish with the beef on top.
4. Heat the remaining oil in the frypan and saute the tomatoes, garlic, salt, pepper, basil and parsley. Cook over a low heat for ten minutes stirring frequently. Spoon over the beef. Sprinkle with the bread crumbs.
5. Bake in a 350°F (180°C) oven for 35 minutes.

Serves 6.

Potato-Beef Pie

2 lb (1 kg) ground beef
3 tablespoons (60 g) melted
   butter or margarine
2½ teaspoons salt
½ teaspoon black pepper
¼ teaspoon marjoram

2 medium carrots, sliced
3 white onions, quartered
   and lightly browned
4 potatoes, thinly sliced
1 cup (150 g) grated cheddar
   cheese

1. Mix together the beef, butter, 1½ teaspoons salt, ¼ teaspoon pepper and the marjoram.
2. Spread half the mixture in a buttered casserole dish.
3. Arrange the carrots, onions and potatoes over it. Cover with the remaining meat mixture.
4. Sprinkle with the remaining salt and pepper and bake in a 325°F (160°C) oven for 45 minutes.
5. Sprinkle the cheese on top and bake for fifteen minutes longer.

Serves 6.

Liver in Wine

2 tablespoons oil
3 large onions
¼ teaspoon saffron
pinch of cayenne
1½ teaspoons paprika
2 tablespoons chopped parsley
1 cup (210 g) brown rice
(uncooked)

2 cups (500 ml) beef stock
6 slices bacon
1 lb (500 g) calves or lambs
liver, sliced
3 tablespoons flour
2 tablespoons lemon juice
½ cup (125 ml) water
¾ (186 ml) white wine

1. Put oil in a casserole dish over a low heat. Slice the onions into it. Add saffron, cayenne, paprika, parsley and rice. Stir constantly while rice is browning — about 10 minutes.
2. Add beef stock and cook, covered, for about 45 minutes until rice is thoroughly cooked.
3. Flour liver. Fry bacon until almost crisp. Remove from frypan and drain. Fry liver in bacon fat until almost cooked. Lay liver on top of rice.
4. Make a gravy by adding flour, lemon juice, water and white wine to the fat left in the frypan. Pour over the liver and rice. Lay bacon on top and bake in a 400°F (200°C) oven, uncovered, for 10-15 minutes.

Serves 4.

Ragout of Beef

3 lb (1½ kg) blade steak, cut
into cubes
2 large onions, chopped
½ cup (125 g) butter or
margarine
2 bay leaves
½ lb (250 g) mushrooms, sliced

1 green pepper, chopped
2 large tomatoes, peeled and
sliced
2 cloves garlic, crushed
salt, pepper and paprika
flour

1. Brown the onions in the butter or margarine in a large saucepan.
2. Add the meat and bay leaves. Half cover with water. Cover and simmer for one hour.
3. Add mushrooms, green pepper, tomatoes and garlic. Season to taste with salt, pepper and paprika. Continue to simmer until the meat is tender.
4. Thicken gravy with flour blended with water.

Serves 6.

Hungarian Beef Goulash

1½ lb (750 g) chuck steak, cut
   into one-inch (2½ cm) cubes
2 tablespoons (40 g) butter
   or margarine
2 medium onions, chopped
1 clove garlic, crushed
3 teaspoons paprika

pinch of marjoram
1½ teaspoons salt
1 medium green pepper, chopped
3 medium tomatoes, peeled and
   quartered
4 medium potatoes, diced

1. In a large saucepan, melt the butter or margarine and saute the onions until transparent.
2. Add the steak, garlic, paprika, marjoram and salt. Cook, stirring frequently, until meat is browned.
3. Cover with water and simmer for about 1½ hours. Add more water if necessary.
4. Add green pepper, tomatoes and potatoes, cover and cook for another 1½-2 hours. Add more salt if needed. Serve with rice or noodles.

Serves 4-6.

Rosemary Beef Casserole

2 lb (1 kg) blade steak, cut
   into cubes
flour seasoned with salt
   and pepper
2 tablespoons oil
3 medium onions, quartered
1 can (425 g) whole tomatoes
1 green pepper, sliced

3 sprigs of fresh rosemary
2 cloves garlic, crushed
1 bay leaf
1 teaspoon dry mustard
1 can (425 g) tomato soup
½ cup (125 ml) water
chopped parsley

1. Coat meat with seasoned flour. Heat oil in a frypan and brown meat on all sides. Put into a casserole dish.
2. Saute the onions in the same frypan, adding more oil if necessary. Add to the meat with the tomatoes, pepper, rosemary, garlic, bay leaf and mustard.
3. Mix the tomato soup with ½ cup water and pour over meat and vegetables. Stir to mix.
4. Cover and cook in a 350°F (180°C) oven for 2½-3 hours.
5. Sprinkle with chopped parsley and serve with rice.

Serves 6.

Beef and Sauerkraut

3 lb (1½ kg) chuck steak,
   cut into bite-size pieces
2 large onions, chopped
2 tablespoons oil
3 teaspoons salt

½ teaspoon pepper
1 teaspoon paprika
1½ lb (750 g) sauerkraut, drained
1 cup (250 ml) boiling water
1 bay leaf

1. Heat the oil in a large saucepan. Saute the onions until transparent. Brown the meat on all sides.
2. Add the salt, pepper and paprika, cover and cook over a low heat for 20 minutes, stirring occasionally.
3. Add the sauerkraut to the meat and onions and cook for ten minutes. Add the boiling water and the bay leaf, cover and cook for about 1½ hours or until meat is cooked well. Remove bay leaf before serving.

Serves 8.

Sweet and Sour Beef

3 lb (1½ kg) blade steak,
   cut into bite-size pieces
2 tablespoons oil
4 onions, chopped

1½ teaspoons salt
3 cups (750 ml) boiling water
4 tablespoons lemon juice
3 tablespoons brown sugar

1. Heat the oil in a large saucepan and brown the meat. Add the onion and cook until they are soft.
2. Add the salt and boiling water and cook, covered, for two hours.
3. Add the lemon juice and brown sugar, mix well, cover and cook for another hour. (Add more sugar if a sweeter taste is desired; more lemon if a sour taste is preferred.) Serve with fluffy rice.

Serves 6-8.

Liver and Bacon Pie

½ lb (250 g) bacon
½ lb (250 g) calf or lamb
  liver
4 onions, sliced
1½ lb (750 g) potatoes, peeled
  and sliced

1 teaspoon dried sage
salt and pepper
beef stock
butter or margarine

1. Cut the bacon and liver into small pieces.
2. Grease a casserole dish and place a layer of potatoes on the bottom, then a layer of onions and a layer of bacon and liver. Sprinkle the meat with sage, salt and pepper. Continue until all the ingredients are used, ending with a layer of potatoes.
3. Pour in a little stock, dot with butter or margarine, cover and cook for one hour in a 350°F (180°C) oven. Remove cover and bake for another 20-30 minutes to brown potatoes.

Serves 4.

Steak and Kidney Hotpot

2 lb (1 kg) steak and kidney
seasoned flour
½ lb (250 g) mushrooms, quartered
1 lb (500 g) carrots, sliced
1 onion, chopped

1 lb (500 g) potatoes, peeled
  and cubed
1 tablespoon tomato paste
1 cup (250 ml) water
salt and pepper

1. Cut up the steak and kidney and coat with the seasoned flour.
2. Put the meat and vegetables in a casserole dish in layers.
3. Mix the tomato paste with the water and pour over the meat and vegetables.
4. Cover and cook in a 350°F (180°C) oven for 2½ hours. Before serving season to taste with salt and pepper.

Serves 6.

Barcelona Beef Stew

     3 lb (1½ kg) rump steak
     6 slices bacon
     2 teaspoons salt
     ½ teaspoon pepper
     3 onions, sliced
     1 cup (210 g) uncooked rice
     1 cup (250 ml) dry white wine
     2 cups (500 ml) beef stock
     1 bay leaf, finely crushed
     ½ teaspoon thyme
     2 cloves garlic, crushed
     ¼ teaspoon saffron
     1½ cups peeled chopped tomatoes

1. Cut the beef into pieces about one inch (2½ cm) thick and two inches (5 cm) square.
2. Cook the bacon in a frypan until crisp. Drain and put in a casserole dish.
3. Brown the meat in the bacon fat. When browned put into the casserole dish with the bacon. Sprinkle with salt and pepper.
4. In the fat remaining in the frypan, saute the onions for five minutes. Add to the meat.
5. In the fat remaining in the frypan, add the rice. Cook over a medium heat, stirring constantly until the rice is lightly browned. Remove rice and reserve.
6. Add the wine to the frypan, bring to a boil, scraping any browned particles from the bottom. Add to the meat with the stock, bay leaf, thyme, garlic and saffron.
7. Cover and bake in a 325°F (160°C) oven for one hour. Add the tomatoes, recover and bake for another 1½ hours.
8. Place the casserole dish over direct heat. Lightly stir in the rice. Cover and cook over a low heat for twenty minutes or until rice is tender. Add more boiling water if necessary.

Serves 6-8.

Beef and Beer Casserole

1½ lb (750 g) chuck steak	1¼ cups (300 ml) beef stock
salt and pepper	1 lb (500 g) onions, sliced
2 tablespoons oil	1 clove garlic, crushed
5 slices bacon	1½ tablespoons sugar
¼ cup flour	1 bouquet garni
1¼ cups (300 ml) beer	3 tablespoons vinegar

1. Cut the meat into bite-size pieces, season with salt and pepper and brown in the hot oil.
2. Add the chopped bacon and cook for five minutes. Remove the meat and bacon and gradually stir in the flour. Brown over a low heat. Gradually add beer and stock, stirring constantly.
3. Place the meat, bacon, sliced onions and garlic in a casserole dish. Sprinkle with sugar. Pour the sauce over and add the bouquet garni.
4. Bake covered in a 300°F (150°C) oven for 3½-4 hours. Before serving remove the bouquet garni and stir in the vinegar.

Serves 4-6.

Swedish Sailor's Stew

1½ lb (750 g) chuck steak, cut into cubes	3 sliced onions
2 lb (1 kg) potatoes, cubed	salt and pepper
2 tablespoons butter or margarine	2 cups (500 ml) boiling water
	2 tablespoons chopped parsley

1. Heat the butter or margarine in a large saucepan and saute the onions until golden brown.
2. Add the meat and brown on all sides.
3. Add the potatoes, salt and pepper to taste, boiling water and parsley. Mix well.
4. Cover tightly and cook over a gentle heat for 3 hours or until the meat is tender.

Serves 4-6.

Hotpot

1 lb (500 g) stewing steak
2 tablespoons oil
1 onion, chopped
1 stalk celery, sliced

½ lb (250 g) carrots, sliced
½ green pepper, chopped
1 orange
salt and pepper

1. Cut the steak into cubes and brown in the hot oil. Put meat in a casserole dish.
2. Saute the onion and celery in the oil until the onion is golden brown.
3. Put the onion, celery, carrots and pepper in the casserole with the meat.
4. Squeeze the juice from half the orange and grate the rind. Mix the juice and rind with the meat and vegetables. Add salt and pepper and half cover with water.
5. Slice the remaining half orange in slices. Arrange these on top of the hotpot. Cover and cook in a 350°F (180°C) oven for two hours, or until meat is tender. Add more water if necessary.

Serves 4.

Spicy Steak Casserole

1½ lb (750 g) round steak
1½ tablespoons plain flour
2 tablespoons brown sugar
1 teaspoon salt
½ teaspoon mixed spice
½ teaspoon ginger
1 teaspoon dry mustard
¼ teaspoon curry powder
¼ teaspoon nutmeg

juice of one lemon
½ cup (125 ml) medium sherry
¼ cup (62.5 ml) tomato sauce
1 tablespoon vinegar
1½ tablespoons Worcestershire sauce
1 beef stock cube
grated rind of ½ lemon
½ lb (250 g) prunes, pitted
   and chopped

1. Cut steak into one-inch (2½ cm) cubes.
2. Mix together flour, sugar, salt, mixed spice, ginger, mustard, curry powder and nutmeg. Toss meat in the flour and spice mixture. Place in a casserole dish and allow to stand for several hours or overnight in the refrigerator.
3. Mix together the lemon juice, sherry, tomato sauce, vinegar and Worcestershire sauce. Add beef cube with enough water to cover the meat.
4. Cover and cook in a 300°F (150°C) oven for about 2½ hours. Forty-five minutes before meat is cooked, add grated lemon rind and prunes.

Serves 4-6.

Vegetable Meat Loaf

½ onion, chopped
½ green pepper, chopped
2 cups grated carrots
2 lb (1 kg) coarsely ground veal
½ cup cracker crumbs

1 teaspoon salt
¼ teaspoon black pepper
1 teaspoon Worcestershire sauce
¼ teaspoon dry mustard
½ cup (125 ml) tomato juice

1. Mix onion, green pepper, carrots and ground meat together.
2. Add cracker crumbs, salt, pepper, Worcestershire sauce and mustard. Add tomato juice and blend well.
3. Shape into a loaf and place in an oiled casserole. Cover and bake in a 400°F (200°C) oven for 40 minutes. Uncover and bake for another 20 minutes.

Serves 6.

Veal and Noodle Supreme

2 lb (1 kg) veal, cubed
¼ cup flour
2 teaspoons salt
½ teaspoon pepper
¼ cup (125 g) butter or margarine
1 small onion, sliced
1 cup (250 ml) water

½ lb (250 g) noodles
¼ lb (125 g) fresh mushrooms, sliced
1 teaspoon sesame seeds
1 cup (250 g) sour cream
¼ cup buttered bread crumbs

1. Roll veal in seasoned flour. Brown in butter or margarine.
2. Add onion and water and simmer, covered, for about 1-1½ hours.
3. Cook noodles in boiling salted water until tender. Drain.
4. Mix the meat with the noodles, mushrooms, sesame seeds and sour cream in a casserole dish. Top with buttered bread crumbs and bake in a 300°F (150°C) oven for about 45 minutes.

Serves 6.

Special Beef Stew

4 lb (2 kg) chuck steak, cut into cubes
3 tablespoons oil
4 tablespoons warm sherry
4 zucchini, sliced
5 carrots, sliced
3 onions, chopped
½ lb (250 g) shelled peas
½ lb (250 g) green beans, cut in pieces

½ lb (250 g) mushrooms, sliced
2 tablespoons flour
4 cups (1 liter) water
salt and pepper
2 bay leaves
red wine
5 tomatoes, peeled and diced

1. Heat oil in a large saucepan and brown meat on all sides. Add sherry and mix well. Remove meat.
2. Put zucchini, carrots, onions, peas, beans and mushrooms in the saucepan and cook briskly for ten minutes, stirring frequently. Add tomato paste and flour and mix well. Stir in water and cook until it boils.
3. Return meat to the saucepan with the vegetables. Season to taste with salt and pepper. Add the bay leaves.
4. Cover and cook very slowly until the meat is tender, about 2½ hours. Add one or two tablespoons of red wine every fifteen minutes during the cooking.
5. When the meat is nearly cooked, add tomatoes.

Serves 8.

Beef in Sesame Seed Sauce

2 lb (1 kg) fillet of beef, cut into one-inch (2½ cm) cubes
½ cup sesame seeds
3 onions, finely chopped
½ cup (125 ml) soy sauce

2 tablespoons brown sugar
1 clove garlic, crushed
¼ cup (62.5 ml) oil
1 lb (500 g) green peas, cooked

1. Brown the sesame seeds in a saucepan. Mix together the sesame seeds, onions, soy sauce, sugar, garlic and half the oil. Marinate the beef in this mixture for one hour at room temperature. Remove the meat, reserving the sauce.
2. Heat the remaining oil in a frypan. Brown the meat in it over a high heat. Add the marinade and peas. Bring to a boil and cook over medium heat for ten minutes.

Serves 4-6.

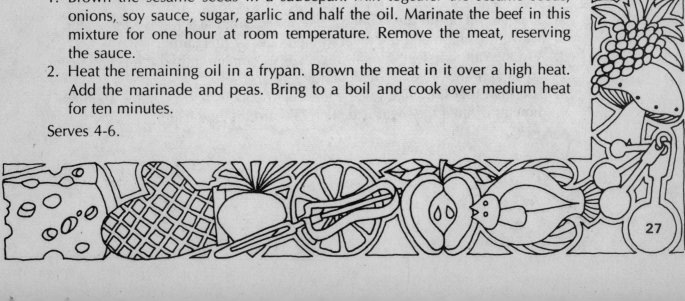

Braised Beef in Beer

4 slices bacon
2 onions, sliced
1 cup chopped celery
2 cups sliced carrots
1 lb (500 g) mushrooms, sliced
3 lb (1½ kg) round steak
2 teaspoons salt

½ teaspoon black pepper
2 teaspoons grated lemon rind
2 cups (500 ml) beer
1 tablespoon flour
2 tablespoons water

1. Place the bacon on the bottom of a heavy saucepan. Spread the onion, celery, carrots and mushrooms over it. Add the meat and sprinkle with the salt, pepper and lemon rind.
2. Cover and cook over a low heat for ½ hour, turning the meat several times.
3. Add the beer, recover and cook for 2½ hours longer.
4. Skim the fat from the gravy. Mix the flour with the water and stir into the gravy until thickened. Cook five minutes longer. Slice the meat and serve with the gravy.

Serves 6-8.

Pot Roast with Prunes and Sweet Potatoes

1 lb (500 g) prunes
2 cups (500 ml) water
1½ cups chopped onions
3 lb (1½ kg) chuck steak
2 tablespoons (40 g) butter or margarine
1½ teaspoon salt

1 bay leaf
3 tablespoons lemon juice
3 tablespoons brown sugar
1 teaspoon cinnamon
1 cup (250 ml) orange juice
3 lb (1½ kg) sweet potatoes, peeled and sliced

1. Soak the prunes in the water for one hour. Drain and reserve the water.
2. Brown the onion and the meat in the butter or margarine.
3. Add the salt, bay leaf, lemon juice, sugar, cinnamon and the prune water. Cover and cook over a low heat for 2 hours.
4. Add the prunes, orange juice and sweet potatoes and cook for another 45 minutes or until the meat is tender. Discard the bay leaf.

Serves 6-8.

Beef Stew in Horseradish Sauce

3 lb (1½ kg) chuck steak, cut
   into bite-size pieces
¼ cup flour
2 teaspoons salt
½ teaspoon pepper
¼ cup (62.5 ml) oil
2 medium onions, minced
1½ cups (375 ml) tomato juice

1 bay leaf
½ teaspoon thyme
3 medium potatoes, cut into
   cubes
½ lb (250 g) peas, cooked
3 tablespoons prepared
   horseradish sauce
1 cup (250 g) sour cream

1. Toss the meat in a mixture of the flour, salt and pepper. Heat the oil in a large saucepan and brown the meat. Add the onions and cook for five minutes.
2. Add the tomato juice, bay leaf and thyme and bring to a boil. Cover and cook over a low heat for two hours.
3. Add the potatoes and peas and cook for another 20 minutes or until the potatoes are cooked.
4. Stir in the horseradish and sour cream. Heat but do not boil. Discard bay leaf.

Serves 6-8.

Tomato and Beef Casserole

2 lb (1 kg) steak, cut
   into bite-size pieces
salt and pepper
2 tablespoons oil
1 large onion, chopped
2 tablespoons flour

1 tablespoon Worcestershire sauce
1½ cups (375 ml) beef stock
2 lb (1 kg) tomatoes, sliced
2 stalks celery, sliced
2 tablespoons chopped parsley

1. Season the steak with salt and pepper and brown on all sides in the hot oil. Add onion and saute until soft.
2. Sprinkle the flour over the steak and onion. Toss thoroughly. Cook for two minutes.
3. Add the Worcestershire sauce and beef stock and bring to a boil, stirring constantly.
4. Put into a casserole dish with the tomatoes and celery. Cover and cook in a 350°F (180°C) oven for 2½-3 hours. Add more salt and pepper if necessary. Garnish with chopped parsley.

Serves 6.

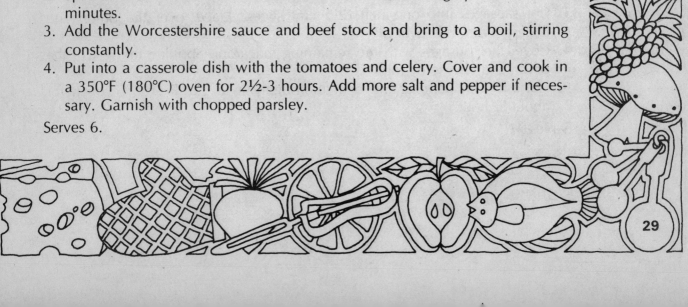

Beef Bourguignon

½ cup (125 g) butter or margarine
6 medium onions, sliced
3 lb (1½ kg) chuck steak, cut into cubes
1 tablespoon flour
1 teaspoon salt

¼ teaspoon pepper
½ teaspoon thyme
½ teaspoon marjoram
2 cups (500 ml) beef stock
1½ cups (375 ml) Burgundy wine
1 lb (500 g) fresh mushrooms

1. Saute the onions in the butter or margarine in a large frypan. Add meat and brown on all sides.
2. Add flour, salt and spices and stir until smooth.
3. Add ½ cup stock and one cup wine and simmer, covered, for three hours.
4. Add mushrooms and continue cooking for another hour.
5. Add the remaining stock and wine as it becomes necessary during cooking.

Serves 6.

Sausage Macaroni Casserole

1 cup (150 g) macaroni
½ teaspoon caraway seeds
½ teaspoon dry mustard
1 onion, chopped
¼ lb (125 g) cheddar cheese, grated

1 lb (500 g) sausages, cooked
¾ cup (186 ml) milk
paprika

1. Cook the macaroni in boiling salted water until tender. Drain. Add the caraway seeds and mustard.
2. Place half the macaroni in a well-buttered casserole dish. Top with half the onion and half the cheese.
3. Cut sausages into one-inch (2½ cm) slices. Place over the onion and cheese. Pour milk over all.
4. Cover the sausages with the remaining macaroni. Sprinkle the rest of the onion and cheese on top.
5. Garnish with paprika and heat thoroughly in a 350°F (180°C) oven for about ½ hour.

Serves 4.

Bulgarian Casserole

1 large eggplant
4 potatoes, cubed
4 tomatoes, quartered
¼ lb (125 g) green beans,
   cut in one-inch (2½ cm) pieces
2 green peppers, chopped
2 lb (1 kg) stewing beef
   or veal

3 tablespoons butter or
   margarine
salt and pepper
2 eggs
1 tablespoon flour
juice of ½ lemon

1. Slice the eggplant, sprinkle with salt and allow to stand for one hour. Drain off the liquid and cut into cubes. Mix with other vegetables.
2. Cut the meat into bite-size pieces and fry gently in the butter or margarine with salt and pepper until it is brown on all sides. Cover with water and simmer for 30 minutes.
3. Put meat and vegetables in a casserole dish with a little more water, cover and cook in a 300°F (150°C) oven for two hours.
4. Beat the eggs with the flour, lemon juice and a little salt. Pour over the casserole and cook uncovered until the eggs are set.

Serves 6.

Old Fashioned Beef Stew

2 lb (1 kg) round or chuck
   steak, cut into cubes
butter, margarine or bacon
   fat
¼ cup flour
salt and pepper
1 clove garlic, crushed

1 teaspoon thyme
3 cups (750 ml) beef stock
2 tablespoons chopped parsley
1 tablespoon chopped celery leaves
1 onion, chopped
1 bay leaf

1. Roll the meat in the flour seasoned with salt and pepper.
2. Heat some fat in a large saucepan and brown the meat on all sides.
3. Stir in the garlic, thyme and beef stock. Mix well and bring to a boil.
4. Add parsley, celery leaves, onion and bay leaf. Cover and simmer gently for 2½ hours or until meat is tender. Correct seasoning.

Serves 6.

Rich Veal Stew

2 lb (1 kg) stewing beef
cold water
salt and pepper
2 small onions, sliced
1 bouquet garni
2 tablespoons butter or margarine

4 tablespoons flour
2½ cups (625 ml) stock
2 tablespoons cream
1 egg yolk
2 teaspoons lemon juice
chopped parsley

1. Cut the veal into bite-size pieces removing any fat. Put in a saucepan and cover with cold water. Add salt and pepper, onions and bouquet garni. Cover and simmer slowly for one hour.
2. When veal is tender, drain but reserve the stock.
3. Make a white sauce with the butter or margarine, flour and stock.
4. Mix the cream and egg yolk together. Add to the white sauce with the lemon juice. Heat, stirring constantly, but do not boil.
5. Add to the veal, season to taste with salt and pepper. Garnish with chopped parsley.

Serves 6.

Braised Veal Cutlets

8 veal cutlets
½ cup (125 g) butter or
   margarine
½ lb (250 g) ham, chopped
½ onion, chopped
2 tablespoons chopped parsley
salt and pepper
1½ cups (375 ml) red wine

1. Heat the butter or margarine in a frypan and brown the cutlets on both sides. Put in a casserole dish.
2. Saute the ham and onion in the butter. Add parsley and season to taste with salt and pepper. Cover the cutlets with the ham and onion mixture.
3. Add the wine and a little water to half cover the meat. Cover and bake in a 350°F (180°C) oven for 45 minutes to one hour.

Serves 4.

Casseroled Leg of Veal

2 lb (1 kg) leg of veal
4 tablespoons oil
2 cloves garlic, crushed
1 lb (500 g) tomatoes, peeled and
   quartered
salt and pepper
1¼ cup (300 ml) white wine
½ teaspoon rosemary
1 tablespoon lemon rind, grated

1. Cut the meat into small pieces.
2. Heat the oil in a casserole and saute the garlic until it is lightly browned.
3. Add the meat and cook until the meat is browned.
4. Add the tomatoes, salt and pepper to taste, white wine, rosemary and grated lemon rind.
5. Cover and cook in a 350°F (180°C) for about an hour.

Serves 4-6.

Veal Shank Stew

3 tablespoons oil
1 clove garlic, chopped
4 veal shanks
3 tablespoons flour
½ cup (125 ml) dry white wine

1 cup (250 ml) water
¼ teaspoon Tabasco sauce
6 strips lemon peel
3 anchovy fillets, chopped
¼ cup chopped parsley

1. Heat oil in a frypan. Add garlic and saute.
2. Roll veal shanks in seasoned flour. Add veal to frypan and brown, turning occasionally. Pour wine and water over all. Stir in Tabasco sauce.
3. Cover frypan and cook over a low heat for about one hour. Add more water if necessary.
4. During the last ten minutes of cooking, add lemon peel and anchovy. Garnish with chopped parsley.

Serves 4.

Special Veal Casserole

2 lb (1 kg) stewing veal
salt and pepper
4 tablespoons flour
2 tablespoons (40 g) butter
  or margarine
2 tablespoons olive oil
1 clove garlic, crushed
¼ cup (62.5 ml) tomato paste

2½ cups (625 ml) beef stock
1 bay leaf
pinch of thyme
pinch of marjoram
¼ lb (125 g) black olives,
  stoned
¼ lb (125 g) mushrooms, sliced

1. Cut the veal into bite-size pieces, toss in the seasoned flour and brown in the butter and oil with the garlic.
2. Add the tomato paste, beef stock, bay leaf, thyme and marjoram and mix well. Put into a casserole dish, cover and bake in a 350°F (180°C) oven for 1½-2 hours. A half hour before the end of cooking time add the olives and mushrooms.

Serves 6.

Veal Hotpot

1 lb (500 g) veal steak
seasoned flour
grated rind of one lemon
½ teaspoon mixed herbs
3 carrots, sliced
1 onion, chopped
¼ lb (125 g) peas, shelled
1 lb (500 g) potatoes, sliced
salt and pepper
chicken stock

1. Cut the meat into cubes and cover each cube with seasoned flour.
2. Put in a casserole and sprinkle with grated lemon rind and mixed herbs.
3. Add the vegetables, cover with potatoes, and half cover with the stock.
4. Cover and cook in a 350°F (180°C) oven for about 1¼ hours.

Serves 4.

Marinated Pot Roast

4 lb (2 kg) round steak, in
   one piece
2½ teaspoons salt
½ teaspoon black pepper
2 medium onions, sliced
2 medium carrots, sliced
2 cloves garlic, sliced
2 teaspoons thyme
⅓ cup chopped parsley
2 bay leaves

1 bottle dry red wine
¼ cup (62.5 ml) brandy
¼ cup (62.5 ml) olive oil
2 tablespoons vegetable oil
1½ cups (375 ml) beef stock
4 white onions, quartered
4 carrots, quartered
1 tablespoon cornstarch
2 tablespoons port wine

1. Rub the meat with the salt and pepper. Spread half the sliced onions, carrots, garlic, thyme, parsley and bay leaves in a large bowl. Put the meat in the bowl and cover with the remaining vegetables and herbs. Mix together the wine, brandy and olive oil. Pour over the meat. Cover and marinate in the refrigerator for 24 hours, or 4 hours at room temperature. Turn and baste frequently. Drain the meat and dry thoroughly. Heat the marinade.
2. Heat the vegetable oil in a flame-proof casserole dish. Brown the meat on all sides.
3. Pour off the fat. Add the heated marinade. Cook over high heat until reduced to half.
4. Add the beef stock and bring to a boil. Cover and bake in a 325°F (160°C) for three hours, turning the meat several times. Add the onions and carrots, re-cover and bake for another 30 minutes. Discard bay leaves.
5. Mix the cornstarch with the port until smooth. Stir into the gravy until thickened.

Serves 8.

Pot Roast, Swedish Style

1 tablespoon salt
1 teaspoon freshly ground pepper
4 lb (2 kg) round steak, in one piece
2 tablespoons (40 g) butter or margarine
2 cups (500 ml) beef stock

2 medium onions, chopped
4 anchovies, minced
2 bay leaves
2 tablespoons vinegar
1 tablespoon brown sugar
6 potatoes, peeled and quartered
½ cup (125 ml) cream
2 tablespoons brandy

1. Rub the salt and pepper into the meat. Melt the butter or margarine in a large saucepan and brown the meat in it. Remove the meat.
2. Stir the stock into the pan and bring to a boil.
3. Mix in the onions, anchovies, bay leaves, vinegar and sugar and return the meat. Cover and cook over a low heat for two hours.
4. Add the potatoes and cook until the potatoes are tender.
5. Stir in the cream and brandy.

Serves 8.

Beef in Lemon Sauce

1 cup fine egg noodles
4 tablespoons (80 g) butter or margarine
1 large onion, chopped
2 lb (1 kg) ground beef
1 lb (500 g) mushrooms, sliced
2 teaspoons salt

½ teaspoon black pepper
¼ teaspoon nutmeg
¾ cup (186 ml) water
2 egg yolks
3 tablespoons lemon juice
2 tablespoons dry sherry

1. Cover the noodles with boiling water and let stand for twenty minutes. Drain.
2. Melt the butter in a saucepan and saute the onion for five minutes.
3. Add the beef, mushrooms and noodles and cook over a high heat, stirring constantly.
4. Add the salt, pepper, nutmeg and water. Cook over low heat for ten minutes.
5. Beat the egg yolks, lemon juice and sherry in a bowl. Add a little of the meat mixture, stirring constantly to prevent curdling. Return to the saucepan. Heat through but do not boil.

Serves 6.

Beef and Rice Stew in Sour Cream Sauce

½ cup (62.5 ml) vegetable oil
3 lb (1½ kg) chuck steak, cut into bite-size pieces
2 teaspoons salt
½ teaspoon black pepper
1 onion, chopped
1 cup (250 ml) tomato juice
1 bay leaf

½ teaspoon marjoram
1½ cups (315 g) uncooked rice
2½ cups (625 ml) boiling beef stock
1 tablespoon prepared horseradish sauce
1 cup (250 g) sour cream

1. Heat the oil in a large saucepan and brown the meat. Season with salt and pepper.
2. Stir in the onions until lightly browned.
3. Add the tomato juice, bay leaf and marjoram. Cover and cook over a low heat for 2 hours.
4. Add the rice, stock and cook for another twenty minutes.
5. Blend in the horseradish and sour cream. Reheat but do not boil.

Serves 6-8.

Beef Stew in Black Sauce

3 lb (1½ kg) chuck steak, cut into serving-sized pieces
¼ cup (62.5 ml) oil
3 onions, sliced
2½ teaspoons salt
½ teaspoon freshly ground black pepper

¼ cup (62.5 ml) lemon juice
½ cup (75 g) currants
3 cups (750 ml) water
4 potatoes, peeled and sliced
4 carrots, quartered
½ cup (75 g) sliced black olives
1 tablespoon capers

1. Heat the oil in a large saucepan. Brown the meat and the onions.
2. Add the salt, pepper, lemon juice, currants and water. Cover and cook over a low heat for two hours.
3. Add the potatoes, carrots, olives and capers and cook for another 45 minutes.

Serves 6-8.

Veal-Beef-Pork Casserole

3 tablespoons vegetable oil
1 lb (500 g) boneless beef,
   cut into one-inch (2½ cm) cubes
½ lb (250 g) boneless veal,
   cut into one-inch (2½ cm) cubes
1 lb (500 g) boneless pork,
   cut into one-inch (2½ cm) cubes
½ cup (105 g) uncooked rice

3 white onions, quartered
1½ cups (375 ml) beef stock
3 potatoes, peeled and sliced
2 carrots, sliced
2 tomatoes, quartered
1 green pepper, sliced
2 teaspoons salt
½ teaspoon black pepper

1. Heat the oil in a flame-proof casserole. Brown the meat in it. Remove the meat.
2. To the remaining fat, add the rice and onions. Cook until the onions are golden brown, stirring frequently.
3. Add the stock and bring to a boil. Return the meat with the potatoes, carrots, tomatoes, green pepper, salt and pepper.
4. Bake in a 350°F (180°C) oven for two hours.

Serves 6-8.

Braised Beef with Ham

3 lb (1½ kg) chuck steak,
   cut into one-inch (2½ cm) cubes
4 tablespoons flour
• ¼ cup (62.5 ml) oil
3 onions, chopped
2 cloves garlic, minced
½ lb (250 g) finely diced ham
1 tablespoon chopped parsley

1 bay leaf
½ teaspoon basil
2 teaspoons salt
½ teaspoon pepper
1 cup (250 ml) beef stock
1½ cups (375 ml) dry white wine
3 green peppers, cut julienne

1. Toss the meat in the flour. Heat the oil in a flame-proof casserole and brown the meat in it.
2. Add the onions, garlic, ham, parsley, bay leaf, basil, salt and pepper and cook for five minutes.
3. Stir in the stock and the wine. Cover and bake in a 275°F (140°C) for two hours. Add the green pepper and bake for another ½ hour or until the meat is tender.

Serves 6-8.

Chicken and Beef Casserole

1 lb (500 g) round steak, cut into one-inch (2½ cm) cubes
1 kg (2 lb) chicken pieces, boned, cut into cubes
½ cup (125 ml) oil
3 onions, chopped
2 green peppers, cut julienne style
2 cloves garlic, crushed

¼ lb (125 g) ham, cut into strips
1 lb (500 g) tomatoes, sliced
½ lb (250 g) Italian sausage, sliced
2 cups (420 g) uncooked rice
4 cups (1 liter) chicken stock
1½ teaspoons salt
½ teaspoon black pepper
1 teaspoon saffron

1. Heat the oil in a flame-proof casserole dish. Saute the onions and peppers for ten minutes.
2. Add the garlic, chicken, beef and ham and cook over a low heat for ten minutes, stirring frequently.
3. Add the tomatoes and cook for five minutes. Add the rice and sausage and cook for another five minutes, shaking the pan frequently.
4. Add the stock, salt, pepper and saffron and bring to a boil. Cook over a high heat for three minutes. Cover, reduce heat and cook for fifteen minutes. Add more stock if saucepan becomes dry.
5. Place uncovered in a 350°F (180°C) oven for 15 minutes.

Serves 6-8.

Beef, Sweet Potato & Pineapple Casserole

3 lb (1½ kg) brisket of beef
1 tablespoon oil
1 onion, chopped
2 teaspoons salt
½ teaspoon black pepper

1 lb (500 g) sweet potatoes, peeled and sliced
⅓ cup brown sugar
2½ cups (625 ml) water
1 large can pineapple pieces

1. Cut the meat into one-inch (2½ cm) slices. Heat the oil in a flame-proof casserole dish. Brown the meat and the onions in it.
2. Mix the salt, pepper, sweet potatoes, sugar and water. Bring to a boil. Cover and bake in a 350°F (180°C) oven for 2½ hours. Add a little more water if necessary.
3. Add the undrained pineapple and bake for twenty minutes longer.

Serves 6-8.

Beef Stew with Dumplings

4 tablespoons oil
3 lb (1½ kg) round steak,
   cut into 6 pieces
3 onions, chopped
1 cup flour
2 cups (500 ml) beef stock
2 tablespoons vinegar
½ teaspoon thyme
½ teaspoon freshly ground
   black pepper

2½ teaspoons salt
¾ teaspoon baking powder
¼ teaspoon marjoram
3 tablespoons chopped parsley
pinch cayenne
3 tablespoons (60 g) butter
   or margarine
2 tablespoons ice water
1½ cups sliced carrots.

1. Heat the oil in a large saucepan. Lightly brown the meat in it. Remove the meat.
2. In the oil remaining in the saucepan, saute the onions for ten minutes. Blend in three tablespoons of the flour until smooth.
3. Gradually add the stock, stirring constantly, until it boils.
4. Add the vinegar, thyme, pepper, 2 teaspoons salt and the meat. Cover and cook over low heat for 2 hours.
5. Sift the remaining flour, salt and the baking powder into a bowl. Add the marjoram, parsley and cayenne, mixing well. Cut in the butter with the pastry blender or two knives until well blended. Add the ice water and toss lightly until a ball of dough is formed. Shape into six balls and drop into the stew with the carrots.
6. Cover and cook over low heat for 30-40 minutes.

Serves 6.

Chicken

Oriental Chicken with Rice

3 lb (1½ kg) chicken pieces
3 cups (750 ml) boiling water
1 onion, chopped
3 tablespoons soy sauce
½ teaspoon white pepper
2 tablespoons cornstarch
2 tablespoons oil

1 cup (210 g) raw rice
1½ cups (375 ml) cold water
1½ teaspoons salt
½ cup (83 g) seedless raisins
½ cup (57 g) slivered toasted almonds
¼ cup shredded coconut

1. Put the chicken pieces, boiling water, onion, soy sauce and pepper in a saucepan. Bring to a boil. Reduce heat and cook over a low heat for 45 minutes or until chicken is tender. Remove the chicken and strain the broth. Return 1¼ cups (300 ml) of the broth to the saucepan and reserve the rest.
2. Mix the cornstarch with 2 tablespoons cold water. Stir into the 1¼ cups broth in the saucepan and cook over a low heat, stirring constantly, until thick and smooth.
3. Heat the oil in a saucepan. Add rice and stir until rice is completely coated with oil. Add 1½ cups cold water, salt and remaining broth. Cover and cook over a low heat until the rice is tender and dry (about 20 minutes).
4. Mix in the raisins and almonds. Add the chicken.
5. Stir in the thickened broth. Sprinkle with the coconut and cook for another ten minutes.

Serves 4-6.

Meal-in-a-Dish Chicken Casserole

2 cups (300 g) macaroni
1 tablespoon (20 g) butter
  or margarine
½ onion, chopped
2 cans condensed cream of
  celery soup
1 cup (250 ml) cream

2½ cups diced cooked chicken
1 small carrot, sliced
½ cup cooked peas
½ cup bread crumbs
3 tablespoons butter
  or margarine, melted
salt and pepper

1. Cook the macaroni in boiling salted water until tender. Drain.
2. Melt one tablespoon butter or margarine in a saucepan. Saute onion until golden brown.
3. Blend in soup and cream, stirring constantly until smooth.
4. Add chicken, carrots and peas and simmer, covered, over a low heat for five minutes.
5. Combine macaroni with chicken and vegetables. Put in a greased casserole dish.
6. Combine bread crumbs with the three tablespoons of butter or margarine and salt and pepper. Sprinkle over casserole and bake in a 375°F (190°C) for 20 minutes.

Serves 4-6.

Chicken Paprika

4 lb (2 kg) chicken pieces
flour
2 teaspoons salt
pepper
1½ teaspoons paprika
ground ginger
½ cup (125 g) butter or
  margarine

2 cups (500 ml) chicken stock
2 cups (500 g) sour cream
1 onion, grated
2 tablespoons chili sauce
1 tablespoon Worcestershire sauce

1. Sprinkle chicken with flour mixed with salt, pepper, paprika and ginger. Saute in butter or margarine until golden brown.
2. Add stock and one cup of sour cream. Mix well. Add the onion, chili sauce and Worcestershire sauce.
3. Cover and cook for 1½ hours. Skim off any excess fat. Add remaining sour cream and cook until chicken is tender. If necessary, thicken with a tablespoon of flour mixed with a little water.

Serves 6-8.

Chicken-Rice Casserole

3 cups cooked rice (1 cup uncooked)
¼ lb (125 g) canned pimientos, chopped
1½ cups diced, cooked chicken

¼ lb (125 g) mushrooms, sliced
½ cup (80 g) blanched almonds
2 cups (500 ml) chicken stock
1½ tablespoons flour
salt and pepper

1. Combine rice and pimientos. Place ⅓ of the rice mixture in a well-buttered casserole dish.
2. Alternate layers of remaining rice, chicken, mushrooms and almonds.
3. Blend flour with chicken stock. Season to taste with salt and pepper and pour over casserole.
4. Bake in a 350°F (180°C) oven for one hour.

Serves 6.

Chicken Curry

2 onions chopped
4 tablespoons oil
4 teaspoons ground coriander
1½ teaspoons cumin
1½ teaspoons dry mustard
1¼ teaspoons tumeric
1 teaspoon cardamon

½ teaspoon ginger
3 lb (1½ kg) chicken legs and breasts
3 teaspoons salt
1½ cups (375 ml) hot water
⅓ cup (83 ml) cream
2 teaspoons lemon juice

1. Saute the onions in the oil until transparent. Mix all the spices together and mix in with the onion. Cook for one minute.
2. Add the chicken to the onion and spices. Stir and cook for five minutes. Add salt and hot water.
3. Cover and cook for 30 minutes. Remove cover and cook for a further 15 minutes or until chicken is tender and water is reduced. Just before serving, stir in the cream. Heat but do not boil. Add lemon juice.

Serves 6.

Chicken Vermouth with Wine

3 lb (1½ kg) chicken pieces	2 cloves garlic, crushed
2½ teaspoons salt	2 tablespoons chopped parsley
½ teaspoon pepper	½ cup (125 ml) white vermouth
3 medium carrots, sliced	¼ cup (62.5 g) sour cream
2 stalks celery, sliced	3 cups hot cooked rice, cooked
1 medium onion, thinly sliced	in chicken stock

1. Sprinkle chicken with salt and pepper.
2. Place all ingredients except sour cream and rice into a casserole dish. Cover with aluminum foil. Place casserole lid over foil.
3. Bake for 1½ hours in a 375°F (190°C) oven. Stir in sour cream and serve over hot rice.

Serves 4.

Chicken with Pineapple

⅔ cup flour	1 large can sliced pineapple
2 teaspoons salt	2 tablespoons lemon juice
¼ teaspoon pepper	2 tablespoons soy sauce
4 lb (2 kg) chicken pieces	
½ cup (125 g) butter	
or margarine	

1. Mix together flour, salt and pepper. Roll chicken pieces in the seasoned flour.
2. Melt butter or margarine in a frypan. Add chicken and cook until lightly browned.
3. Drain pineapple. Measure 1½ cups (375 ml) pineapple syrup and mix with lemon juice and soy sauce.
4. Place chicken in a casserole dish. Pour pineapple syrup mixture over chicken.
5. Cover and bake in a 350°F (180°C) oven for 1½ hours. Add pineapple slices for the last 20 minutes of cooking. Bake uncovered after adding pineapple slices.

Serves 6.

Chicken Pie

1 cup diced cooked chicken
2 tablespoons butter or
  margarine (40 g)
2 tablespoons flour
1 teaspoon salt
¼ teaspoon pepper
½ cup (125 ml) milk
½ cup (125 ml) cream

Dough:
2 cups flour
4 teaspoons baking powder
½ teaspoon salt
4 tablespoons (80 g) butter
  or margarine
⅔ cup (166 ml) milk

1. Melt butter or margarine in a saucepan. Add two tablespoons flour, salt and pepper. Add milk and cream, stirring constantly, and cook until thick and smooth.
2. Make dough by adding together the flour, baking powder, salt, butter or margarine and milk. Roll out half the dough and line a shallow casserole dish.
3. Put chicken in casserole and pour white sauce over.
4. Roll out remaining dough and cut into 2-inch (5 cm) rounds. Place rounds on top of casserole.
5. Bake in a 400°F (200°C) oven for 30 minutes.

Serves 4.

Sweet Potato Chicken Pie

4 lb (2 kg) chicken pieces
4 tablespoons butter or margarine
½ cup chopped celery
5 tablespoons flour
1 bay leaf
3 whole cloves

2 cups (500 ml) chicken broth
½ cup (125 ml) milk
1 cup peas
salt and pepper
2 cups mashed sweet potatoes

1. Cook chicken until tender and remove meat from bones.
2. Melt butter or margarine in the top of a double boiler. Add celery and cook until tender. Place over boiling water, add flour and stir until well blended. Add bay leaf and cloves. Gradually add the chicken broth and milk. Cook, stirring constantly, until mixture thickens. Remove spices. Add peas and season to taste with salt and pepper.
3. Put chicken in a casserole. Pour sauce over the chicken. Spread mashed sweet potatoes over the top.
4. Bake in a 400°F (200°C) oven for 15-10 minutes.

Serves 6.

Chicken-Rice Curry

4 tablespoons (80 g) butter
   or margarine
1½ teaspoons salt
¼ teaspoon white pepper
curry powder to taste
2 lb (1 kg) chicken pieces

1 cup (115 g) slivered blanched
   almonds
1 cup (250 ml) cream
1 cup (210 g) uncooked rice
2 cups (500 ml) hot chicken stock

1. Melt the butter or margarine in a flame-proof casserole dish. Stir in salt, pepper and curry powder. Add the chicken and turn the pieces to coat with the seasoned butter. Cook for five minutes.
2. Stir in the almonds and cream.
3. Cover and bake in a 350°F (180°C) oven for 30 minutes. Add the rice and broth and recover. Bake ½ hour longer, uncovering for the last ten minutes.

Serves 4.

Chicken and Cabbage Stew

4 lb (2 kg) chicken pieces
3 tablespoons (60 g) butter
   or margarine
2 tablespoons olive oil
2 onions, chopped
3 cloves garlic, crushed
3 tablespoons chopped parsley
1 cup grated carrots

4 cups shredded cabbage
2 teaspoons salt
½ teaspoon pepper
¾ cup (186 ml) dry white
   wine
4 small potatoes, peeled
   and quartered
½ cup pitted green olives

1. Heat the butter and oil in a large saucepan and brown the chicken. Remove chicken.
2. Put onions, garlic and parsley in dish and saute for ten minutes, stirring frequently.
3. Return the chicken and add the carrots, cabbage, salt and pepper. Cook over a low heat for 15 minutes.
4. Add the wine, potatoes and olives. Cover and cook over a low heat for 45 minutes or until chicken and potatoes are cooked.

Serves 6-8.

Brunswick Stew

2 lb (1 kg) chicken pieces
1½ lb (750 g) stewing beef,
   cut into one-inch cubes
6 cups (1½ liters) water
3 teaspoons salt
½ teaspoon black pepper
1 lb (500 g) canned tomatoes

1 lb (500 g) canned cream-style
   corn
2 potatoes, diced
2 medium onions, chopped
½ cup (105 g) uncooked rice
Pinch cayenne

1. Combine the chicken, beef and water in a large saucepan. Bring to a boil, skim the top and add 2 teaspoons salt and the pepper. Cover and cook over a low heat for one hour.
2. Drain the meat and chicken. Cut the chicken into bite-size pieces discarding the bones.
3. Pour off all but 2 cups of broth. Return the meat and chicken. Add the tomatoes, corn, potatoes, onions, rice and cayenne. Add remaining one teaspoon salt.
4. Cover and cook over low heat for 45 minutes or until beef is tender.

Serves 6-8.

Chicken with Prunes

4 lb (2 kg) chicken pieces
2½ teaspoons salt
½ teaspoon black pepper
4 tablespoons (80 g) butter
   or margarine
1 cup diced carrots

1 onion, chopped
1 lb (500 g) pitted prunes
4 potatoes, peeled and quartered
2 tablespoons lemon juice
1½ cup (375 ml) boiling water

1. Rub chicken with 2 teaspoons of the salt and the pepper.
2. Melt the butter or margarine in a flame-proof casserole dish. Brown the chicken in it.
3. Add the carrots and onion. Cover and bake in a 375°F (190°C) oven for 20 minutes, basting frequently.
4. Add the prunes, potatoes, lemon juice, water and remaining ½ teaspoon salt. Re-cover and bake for another 30-35 minutes or until chicken and potatoes are tender.

Serves 6.

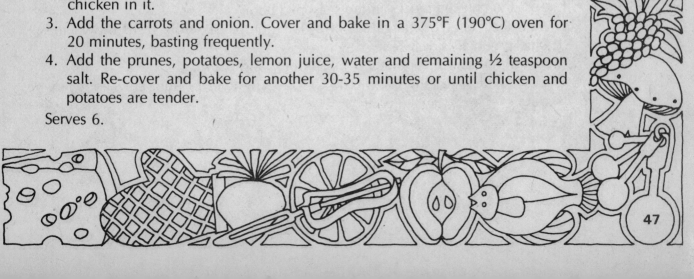

Chicken in Cream

4 lb (2 kg) chicken pieces	1½ teaspoons salt
3 tablespoons (60 g) butter or margarine	½ teaspoon pepper
	½ teaspoon saffron
3 medium onions, sliced	1 bay leaf
3 carrots, sliced	3 potatoes, cubed
½ cup (125 ml) dry sherry	1 egg yolk
1¼ cups (300 ml) chicken stock	1 cup (250 ml) cream

1. Melt the butter or margarine in a flame-proof casserole dish. Brown chicken pieces. Remove.
2. Saute onions and carrots in remaining butter or margarine. Return the chicken and add the sherry, chicken stock, salt, pepper, saffron and bay leaf.
3. Cover and bake in a 350°F (180°C) oven for ½ hour.
4. Add the potatoes, recover and cook for another ½ hour or until potatoes and chicken are tender.
5. Beat the egg yolk and stir in the cream. Add a little of the pan juices, stirring constantly. Pour over the chicken, reheat in the oven for 5 minutes and serve immediately.

Serves 6-8.

Chicken in Sour Cream Sauce

2 lb (1 kg) chicken pieces	1 cup (250 g) sour cream
½ cup flour	1 cup (250 ml) chicken stock
2 teaspoons salt	½ lb (250 g) fresh mushrooms, sliced
¼ teaspoon white pepper	
4 tablespoons (80 g) butter or margarine	1½ teaspoons paprika

1. Toss the chicken pieces in the seasoned flour.
2. Melt the butter or margarine in a flame-proof casserole dish. Brown the chicken on all sides.
3. Mix in the sour cream, stock, mushrooms and paprika.
4. Cover and bake in a 350°F (180°C) for 45 minutes or until chicken is tender.

Serves 4-6.

Braised Chicken with Peas

4 lb (2 kg) chicken pieces
2 teaspoons salt
½ teaspoon black pepper
4 tablespoons (80 g) butter
  or margarine
2 medium onions, chopped
1 clove garlic, crushed
¼ lb (125 g) ham, julienne-cut

¼ teaspoon thyme
1 bay leaf, crushed
2 tablespoons chopped parsley
1½ cups (375 ml) boiling water
1 tablespoon cornstarch
1 cup (250 ml) cream
1 lb (500 g) green peas, cooked
2 potatoes, peeled and diced

1. Season the chicken pieces with salt and pepper.
2. Melt the butter or margarine in a heavy saucepan and saute the chicken for ten minutes, turning often.
3. Add the onions and cook until browned. Mix in the garlic, ham, thyme, bay leaf and parsley and cook for another five minutes, stirring frequently.
4. Add the water, cover and cook over a low heat for one hour.
5. Mix the cornstarch with the cream. Stir into the gravy until the mixture boils. Add the peas and potatoes and cook until potatoes are tender.

Serves 6.

Chicken in Whisky Sauce

4 lb (2 kg) chicken pieces
2 teaspoons salt
½ teaspoon white pepper
½ cup (125 g) butter or
  margarine

½ cup (125 ml) whisky
1 onion, sliced
1 cup grated carrots
2 cups chopped tomatoes
1½ cups (375 ml) cream

1. Season the chicken pieces with salt and pepper.
2. Melt the butter or margarine in a saucepan and brown the chicken on all sides.
3. Add the whisky and cook over a high heat for two minutes. Add the onions, carrots, tomatoes and cream.
4. Bring to a boil, cover and cook over a low heat for ½ hour or until chicken is tender.

Serves 6.

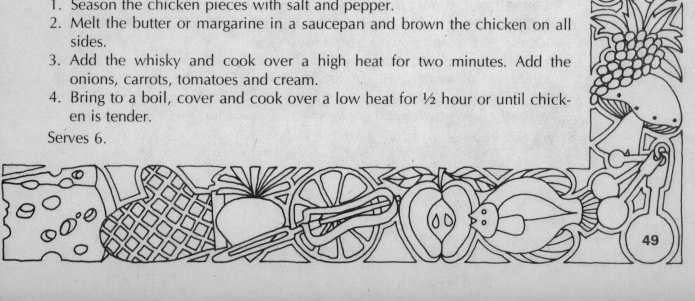

49

Lamb

Spicy Lamb Stew with Dumplings

3 lb (1½ kg) boneless lamb	2½ teaspoons salt
6 onions, chopped	4 tablespoons (80 g) butter
3 cloves garlic, crushed	or margarine
1 teaspoon ground cumin	2 cups (500 ml) water
2 teaspoons ground coriander	2 egg yolks
1½ teaspoons tumeric	2 tablespoons (40 g) melted
½ teaspoon powdered ginger	butter or margarine
½ teaspoon dried ground chili	½ cup wheat meal flour
peppers	2 egg whites, stiffly beaten

1. Cut the lamb in one-inch (2½ cm) cubes.
2. Pound to a paste the onions, garlic, cumin, coriander, tumeric, ginger, chili pepper and two teaspoons salt. Toss the meat in the mixture until coated. Let stand for ½ hour.
3. Melt the four tablespoons butter or margarine in a large saucepan. Cook the meat in it, stirring frequently, until browned.
4. Add half the water. Cover and cook over a low heat for 45 minutes, adding the remaining water from time to time.
5. Make dumplings by beating together the egg yolks, melted butter or margarine and remaining salt. Stir in the flour. Fold in the egg whites. Chill for 15 minutes and shape into walnut-size balls. Arrange dumplings on top of the stew. Cover and cook over a low heat for 25-30 minutes.

Serves 6-8.

Pineapple Lamb Casserole

8 lamb chops
butter or margarine
½ lb (250 g) Italian sausage,
  cut into small pieces

8 slices pineapple
½ lb (250 g) mushrooms
salt and pepper
1½ cups (375 ml) pineapple juice

1. Fry the chops in the butter or margarine until golden brown. Place in a casserole dish.
2. Fry the sausage in the butter for five minutes. Add to the casserole.
3. Place a slice of pineapple on top of each chop.
4. Place mushrooms in the casserole. Season with salt and pepper.
5. Pour the juice over and cover. Cook in a 350°F (180°C) oven for about one hour or until the chops are tender.

Serves 4-8.

Lamb Paprika

2 lb (1 kg) best end
  lamb chops
2 tablespoons (40 g) butter or
  margarine
2 onions, chopped
1 lb (500 g) tomatoes, peeled
  and chopped

1 tablespoon chopped parsley
2 teaspoons paprika
salt
½ cup (125 g) sour cream

1. Heat the butter or margarine in a frypan and brown both sides of meat. Remove from pan.
2. Saute the onions in the frypan until they are golden brown.
3. Put meat and onions in a casserole dish, add tomatoes, parsley, paprika and salt to taste. Mix well and bake, covered, in a 325°F (160°C) oven for two hours.
4. Stir in the sour cream and reheat.

Serves 6.

Curried Lamb

1 lb (500 g) boneless lamb, cut into bite-size pieces	¼ teaspoon allspice
2 cloves	1 bay leaf
curry powder to taste	2 onions, chopped
¼ teaspoon nutmeg	1 lb (500 g) tomatoes, peeled and chopped
¼ teaspoon ground ginger	salt and pepper

1. In a large saucepan, brown the meat in oil.
2. Add the spices and bay leaf and saute for one minute.
3. Add onions, tomatoes, salt and pepper to taste and mix well.
4. Add a little water, cover and simmer for 1-1½ hours. Remove bay leaf before serving.

Serves 4.

North Country Casserole

4 forequarter chops	¼ teaspoon ground cloves
2 tablespoons (40 g) butter or margarine	¼ teaspoon thyme
1 clove garlic, crushed	1 teaspoon salt
4 medium potatoes, quartered	¼ teaspoon pepper
4 small onions, halved	1 can (445 g) condensed mushroom soup
¼ lb (125 g) green beans, cut in one-inch (2½ cm) lengths	½ cup (125 ml) water
	paprika

1. Fry the chops on both sides in the butter or margarine with the garlic.
2. Put chops in a casserole dish with the potatoes and onions.
3. Add the beans, cloves, thyme, salt and pepper, condensed mushroom soup and water. Cover and cook in a 350°F (180°C) oven for one hour. Sprinkle with paprika before serving.

Serves 4.

Lamb and Celery Stew

¼ cup flour
1½ teaspoons salt
⅛ teaspoon black pepper
2 lb (1 kg) stewing lamb,
cut into cubes
2 tablespoons oil
2 small onions, chopped

2 cups (500 ml) boiling water
1 lb (500 g) potatoes, peeled
and quartered
2 small carrots, sliced
3 cups celery, cut into
one-inch (2½ cm) pieces

1. Mix flour with salt and pepper. Toss lamb cubes in the flour.
2. In a large saucepan, heat the oil. Add lamb and brown well.
3. Add onions and saute until lightly browned. Gradually add water.
4. Cover and cook 1½-2 hours, stirring occasionally.
5. Add potatoes and carrots and cook for 15 minutes. Add celery and cook until vegetables and meat are tender.

Serves 6.

Lamb Curry

2 tablespoons (40 g) butter
or margarine
4 lb (2 kg) lean lamb cut
in one-inch (2½ cm) cubes
2 onions, chopped
1 teaspoon salt
1 teaspoon Worcestershire sauce

½ teaspoon prepared mustard
1 bay leaf
2 peppercorns
2 tablespoons tomato sauce
curry powder to taste
2 cups (500 ml) stock

1. Melt the butter or margarine in a large saucepan. Brown the lamb and onions.
2. Combine the salt, Worcestershire sauce, mustard, bay leaf, peppercorns, tomato sauce and curry powder. Mix stock with the seasoning mixture. Add to lamb and blend well.
3. Bring to a boil. Reduce heat and simmer, covered, for two hours or until tender.

Serves 8-10.

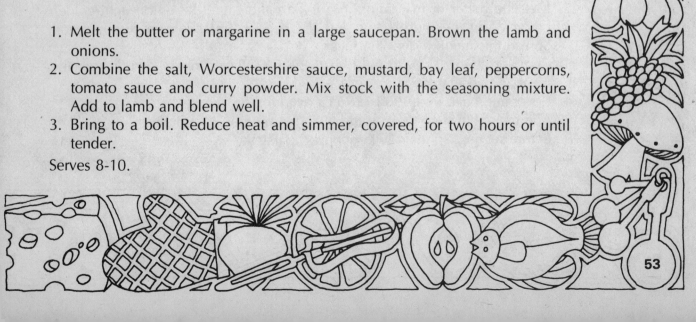

53

Persian Lamb Stew

½ cup dried kidney beans
cold water
2 lb (1 kg) cubed boneless
  lamb shoulder
2 tablespoons oil
½ onion, chopped
2 cups (500 ml) tomato sauce
¼ cup (62.5 ml) water

1 tablespoon lemon juice
1 teaspoon salt
½ teaspoon each oregano,
  thyme, tumeric
¼ teaspoon each coarsely ground
  black pepper, cinnamon
1 bay leaf

1. Soak beans in cold water overnight. Drain. Parboil in boiling salted water to cover for 15 minutes. Drain.
2. In a large saucepan brown lamb in hot oil. Add onion and cook until onion is brown. Stir in beans, tomato sauce, ¼ cup water, lemon juice, salt and seasonings.
3. Bring to a boil. Reduce heat, cover and simmer for 1½ hours or until meat and beans are tender. Skim off any excess fat.

Serves 6.

Roast Lamb Casserole

12 slices cooked lamb
3 onions, sliced
¼ lb (125 g) fresh mushrooms,
  sliced
½ red pepper
2 tablespoons (40 g) butter
  or margarine

1½ cups (375 ml) stock
2 tablespoons paste
1 teaspoon salt
¼ teaspoon pepper
1 cooking apple, peeled and
  sliced
2 tablespoons chopped parsley

1. Place meat in a buttered casserole dish.
2. Melt the butter or margarine in a frypan and saute the onion until golden brown. Add the mushrooms and red pepper and cook for five minutes. Spread this mixture over the meat.
3. Combine the stock with the tomato paste, salt and pepper. Pour over the meat and vegetables.
4. Cover and bake in a 350°F (180°C) oven for 30 minutes.
5. Add the apple slices, cover and bake for another 30 minutes.
6. Before serving, sprinkle with chopped parsley.

Serves 4.

Lamb Stew with Sour Cream

3 lb (1½ kg) lamb shoulder, cut into bite-size pieces	1½ teaspoons paprika
	salt and pepper
4 onions, sliced	3 large tomatoes, sliced
3 tablespoons (60 g) butter	1 cup (250 g) sour cream
or margarine	½ cup chopped parsley

1. Saute the onion in the butter or margarine until golden brown.
2. Add the well-seasoned meat and brown on all sides.
3. Add the tomatoes, cover and cook slowly for two hours. Add just enough water to prevent burning.
4. Just before serving, stir in sour cream and parsley. Heat through.

Serves 6-8.

Pilaf with Lamb Patties

4 slices bacon	**Lamb Patties:**
2 tablespoons prepared mustard	1 lb (500 g) ground lamb
1 cup brown rice	2 tablespoons prepared mustard
1 onion, thinly sliced	1 teaspoon salt
2 cups (500 ml) tomato juice	¼ teaspoon pepper

1. Cut the bacon into small pieces and brown slowly in a frypan. Add two tablespoons mustard and brown rice. Stir over low heat until brown and heated through.
2. Add the onion and tomato juice and bring quickly to a boiling point. Put into casserole dish.
3. Make lamb Patties by combining lamb, mustard, salt and pepper and shaping into patties.
4. Arrange lamb patties on top of rice mixture and bake, uncovered, in a 400°F (200°C) oven until patties are brown on top (about 15 minutes). Cover and bake until rice is well cooked (about 20-30 minutes).

Serves 4.

Lancashire Casserole

2 lb (1 kg) lamb loin chops
½ lb (250 g) mushrooms, sliced
3 onions, sliced
1 lb (500 g) potatoes, peeled
  and sliced
salt and pepper
stock
butter or margarine

1. Cut any excess fat from the chops.
2. Put the meat in the bottom of a casserole dish and cover with a layer of sliced mushrooms, then the onions and lastly the potatoes. Season after each layer.
3. Pour in enough stock to half cover. Dot the potatoes with butter or margarine.
4. Cover and cook in a 325°F (160°C) oven for 2½ to 3 hours. Remove the cover towards the end of the cooking time to brown the potatoes.

Serves 6-8.

Curried Lamb Stew

3 tablespoons (60 g) butter
  or margarine
2 onions, finely chopped
3 lb (1½ kg) boneless lamb,
  cut into one-inch (2½ cm) cubes
2 teaspoons salt

curry powder to taste
¼ cup chopped preserved ginger
1½ cups (375 ml) beef stock
2 tablespoons lemon juice
½ cup (47 g) desiccated coconut
1 cup (250 ml) cream

1. Melt the butter or margarine in a large saucepan. Brown the onions and lamb in it.
2. Stir in the salt, curry powder, ginger and stock. Cover and cook over a low heat for one hour.
3. Stir in the lemon juice, coconut and cream. Cook for ten minutes, but do not boil.

Serves 6-8.

Lamb with Peaches

6 lamb shanks
1½ teaspoons salt
1 teaspoon pepper
1 clove garlic, crushed
1 large onion, chopped
2 cups (500 ml) milk
1 large can sliced peaches,
    drained

4 teaspoons Angostura bitters
½ teaspoon marjoram
pinch of thyme
¼ teaspoon rosemary
⅓ cup (80 g) raisins

1. Rub lamb shanks with salt, pepper and garlic. Place in a large saucepan, cover with boiling water and simmer until almost tender, about 45 minutes. Remove shanks and trim off meat, discarding bones. Cut meat into bite-size pieces.
2. Place lamb in a large saucepan. Add onion and milk. Simmer all together gently until the milk is almost absorbed.
3. Add peaches, bitters, marjoram, thyme, rosemary and raisins. Heat together slowly, stirring occasionally, for about 30 minutes.

Serves 6.

Braised Lamb in Sour Cream

2 lb (1 kg) lamb loin
    chops
¼ cup flour
2 teaspoons salt
¼ teaspoon pepper
pinch of thyme
pinch of tarragon
2 tablespoons butter or
    margarine

1½ cups (375 ml) stock
¼ teaspoon caraway seeds
juice of ½ lemon
1 cup (250 g) sour cream
2 tablespoons white wine
    (optional)

1. Trim the lamb of most of its fat.
2. Mix the flour, salt, pepper, thyme and tarragon. Toss the meat in the flour and brown in the melted butter or margarine in a frypan.
3. Pour stock over the meat. Stir in caraway seeds, lemon juice, sour cream and wine. Mix well.
4. Cover and cook over a very low heat for 1½ hours.

Serves 4-6.

Lamb Pulao

2 cups (420 g) uncooked rice
½ cup (125 g) butter or
    margarine
2 lb (1 kg) boneless lamb, cut
    into one-inch (2½ cm) cubes
2 onions, sliced
2 cloves garlic, crushed
2 teaspoons salt
⅛ teaspoon ground cardamon

2 cloves
1 teaspoon powdered ginger
1 teaspoon cinnamon
1 bay leaf
3 cups (750 g) yoghurt
1 teaspoon saffron
¼ cup (20 g) slivered blanched
    almonds
½ cup seedless raisins

1. Wash the rice, then soak in cold water for twenty minutes. Drain thoroughly.
2. Melt the butter or margarine in a large saucepan. Brown the lamb and onions in it very well.
3. Sprinkle with the garlic, salt, cardamon, cloves, ginger and cinnamon. Mix well.
4. Add the bay leaf and yoghurt. Bring to a boil. Reduce heat, cover and cook for one hour.
5. Dissolve the saffron in a little boiling water and add to the lamb with the rice. If liquid does not cover the rice, add boiling water to barely cover.
6. Cover the saucepan and cook for 20 minutes longer or until the rice is almost tender.
7. Mix in the almonds and raisins and cook for another five minutes or until all the liquid is absorbed.

Serves 6.

Bacon and Lamb Casserole

4 rib lamb chops
1 tablespoon oil
½ lb (250 g) bacon, chopped
4 large onions, sliced
5 large tomatoes, sliced
salt and curry powder to taste

1. Brown the chops in the oil with the bacon.
2. Grease a casserole dish and layer the onions and tomatoes, seasoning with salt and curry powder after each layer.
3. Place the chops on top, cover and bake in a 375°F (190°C) oven for one hour. Remove cover and cook for another 15 minutes.

Serves 4.

Lamb-Vegetable Casserole

4 tablespoons (80 g) butter
  or margarine
3 onions, thinly sliced
2 lb (1 kg) boneless lamb,
  cut into ½-inch (1 cm) cubes
1 cup (250 g) uncooked rice
1 cup (250 g) yoghurt
2 teaspoons ground cumin
1 lb (500 g) green beans, cut
  into one-inch (2½ cm) pieces

1 lb (500 g) green peas, shelled
1 carrot, diced
1 clove garlic, crushed
¼ teaspoon powdered ginger
2 tablespoons tomato paste
2 cups (500 ml) boiling water
2½ teaspoons salt
½ teaspoon black pepper

1. Melt the butter or margarine in a large saucepan. Saute the onions and lamb for ten minutes.
2. Mix in the rice, yoghurt and cumin and cook over a low heat for five minutes.
3. Add the beans, peas and carrot. Cook over a low heat for ten minutes, stirring occasionally.
4. Mix in the garlic, ginger, tomato paste, water, salt and pepper. Cover and cook over a low heat for twenty minutes. Add more water if necessary.

Serves 6.

Swedish Lamb Stew

6 rib chops, cut
  one-inch (2½ cm) thick
3 tablespoons (60 g) butter
  or margarine
3 onions, sliced
2 medium carrots, sliced

1½ teaspoons salt
½ teaspoon black pepper
2 teaspoons brown sugar
1¼ cups (300 ml) coffee
½ cup (125 ml) cream
6 potatoes, peeled and quartered

1. Trim the fat from the chops. Melt the butter or margarine in a large saucepan. Brown the lamb and onions in it. Pour off the fat.
2. Add the carrots, salt and pepper and sugar. Cook for five minutes.
3. Mix in the coffee and cream. Cover and bring to a boil. Reduce heat and cook over a low heat for 45 minutes.
4. Add the potatoes and cook for another 20 minutes.

Serves 6.

Lamb Hot Pot

4 tablespoons (80 g) butter or margarine	3 large onions, sliced
6 rib chops	¼ lb (125 g) mushrooms, sliced
2½ teaspoons salt	½ lb (250 g) green beans, cut in one-inch (2½ cm) pieces
1 teaspoon black pepper	1 cup (250 ml) beef stock
6 potatoes, peeled and sliced	½ cup (125 ml) cream

1. Melt half the butter or margarine in a frypan. Brown chops on both sides. Place in a casserole dish and sprinkle with 1½ teaspoons salt and ½ teaspoon pepper.
2. Arrange a layer of half the potatoes over the chops. Layer the mushrooms, onions and string beans on the top.
3. Mix the stock, cream and remaining salt and pepper. Pour over the vegetables.
4. Arrange the remaining potatoes on top of the vegetables. Dot with the remaining butter.
5. Cover and bake in a 350°F (180°C) oven for 2½ hours. Remove cover and bake for 15 minutes or until potatoes are brown on top.

Serves 6.

Lamb Shanks with Rice

4 lamb shanks	2 medium tomatoes, chopped
3 tablespoons vegetable oil	3 cups (750 ml) water, boiling
3 white onions, quartered	1 cup (210 g) uncooked rice
2 teaspoons salt	1 lb (500 g) green beans, whole
½ teaspoon pepper	3 tablespoons minced parsley
¼ teaspoon marjoram	

1. Heat the oil in a large saucepan. Brown the shanks in it. Pour off the fat.
2. Add the onions and brown well. Add the salt, pepper, marjoram, tomatoes and one cup of the water. Cover and cook over a low heat for 1½ hours.
3. Add the remaining boiling water, the rice and green beans. Re-cover and cook over a low heat for ½ hour. Sprinkle with parsley.

Serves 4.

Lamb and Bean Stew

3 lb (1½ kg) boneless lamb, cut into one-inch (2½ cm) cubes
⅓ cup (83 ml) oil
4 onions, chopped parsley
2½ teaspoons salt
¾ teaspoon black pepper
⅓ cup (83 ml) lemon juice
1 lemon, quartered
3 cups (750 ml) boiling water
2 lb (1 kg) canned kidney beans

1. Heat two tablespoons of the oil in a large saucepan. Brown the lamb in it. Remove the lamb.
2. Heat the remaining oil in the saucepan. Add the onions and parsley and cook for five minutes, stirring frequently.
3. Return the meat and add the salt, pepper, lemon juice, lemon and boiling water.
4. Cover and cook over a low heat for 1¼ hours.
5. Add the undrained beans and cook for another 15-20 minutes.

Serves 6-8.

Lamb and Rice a la Greque

4 tablespoons (80 g) butter or margarine
1½ lb (750 g) boneless lamb, cut into ½-inch (1 cm) cubes
2 onions, chopped
1 clove garlic, crushed
1 cup shredded lettuce
½ lb (250 g) pork sausage, sliced
¼ lb (125 g) sliced mushrooms
2 tomatoes, peeled and diced
1½ cups (315 g) uncooked rice
3 cups (750 ml) boiling water
1½ teaspoons salt
¼ cup peas, cooked
4 tablespoons raisins

1. Melt two tablespoons of the butter or margarine in a large saucepan. Brown the lamb in it. Remove the lamb.
2. Add the remaining butter and saute the onions for ten minutes.
3. Add the garlic, lettuce, sausage, mushrooms and tomatoes. Cook for five minutes, stirring constantly.
4. Return the lamb to the saucepan and cook over a low heat for ½ hour.
5. Mix in the rice. Add the boiling water, salt and pepper.
6. Cover and cook over a low heat for 30 minutes.
7. Stir in the peas and raisins and heat through.

Serves 6-8.

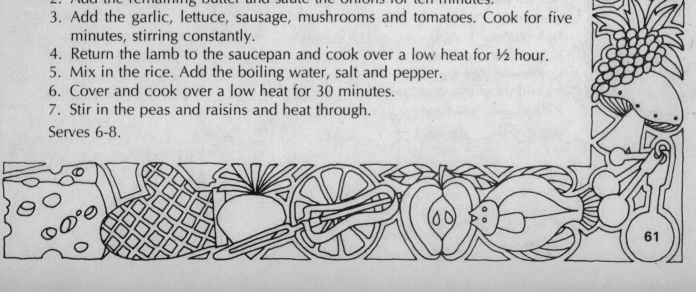

Lamb and Barley Stew

½ cup (105 g) barley
2 cups (500 ml) water
3 tablespoons oil
2 lb (1 kg) boneless lamb,
  cut into one-inch (2½ cm) cubes
2 onions, sliced

½ green pepper, sliced
2 teaspoons salt
¼ teaspoon pepper
3 potatoes, diced
2 carrots sliced
3 tablespoons minced parsley

1. Wash the barley and soak in the two cups of water for one hour.
2. Heat the oil in a large saucepan and brown the lamb in it. Add the onions and saute for five minutes. Pour off the fat.
3. Add the green pepper, salt, pepper and undrained barley. Bring to a boil. Reduce heat, cover and cook over a low heat for 1½ hours. Add a little more boiling water, if necessary.
4. Add the potatoes and carrots, recover and cook for another ½ hour. Sprinkle with the parsley.

Serves 4-6.

Ground Lamb Curry

2 lb (1 kg) lean ground lamb
1 onion, finely chopped
2 cloves garlic, crushed
2½ teaspoons salt
½ cup (125 g) butter or
  margarine

2 onions, thinly sliced
curry powder to taste
1 tablespoon tomato paste
2 cups (500 g) yoghurt
2 potatoes, peeled and cubed
¼ cup (30 g) ground almonds

1. Mix together the lamb, chopped onion, garlic and 1½ teaspoons salt. Shape into one-inch (2½ cm) balls.
2. Melt the butter or margarine in a large saucepan. Saute the sliced onions until golden brown. Add the meat balls and cook for five minutes, turning the meat balls frequently.
3. Mix the curry powder with the tomato paste, yoghurt and remaining salt. Mix into the saucepan with the meat balls. Cook over low heat for ten minutes, stirring frequently.
4. Add the potatoes and almonds. Cover and cook for 20 minutes over a low heat. Add more water if necessary.

Serves 6-8.

Provence Casserole

6 loin chops, cut
  one-inch (2½ cm) thick
1½ lb (750 g) tomatoes, sliced
3 teaspoons salt
½ teaspoon black pepper
1 clove garlic, crushed
½ teaspoon basil
1 medium eggplant, peeled
  and thinly sliced

2 green peppers, cut in
  large strips
1 cup (210 g) uncooked rice
1 cup pureed canned tomatoes
1 cup (250 ml) beef stock
3 tablespoons oil

1. Brown the chops on both sides in a frypan. Drain.
2. In a greased casserole dish, spread half the tomatoes. Sprinkle with a little of the salt, pepper, garlic and basil.
3. Layer half the eggplant and green peppers, seasoning each layer. Repeat the layers.
4. Spread rice over the eggplant and peppers. Arrange chops over the rice and season. Add the pureed tomatoes and stock and sprinkle with the oil.
5. Cover and bake in a 400°F (200°C) oven for 1¼ hours. Add a very little water if necessary to keep from burning. Uncover and bake for ten minutes longer.

Serves 6.

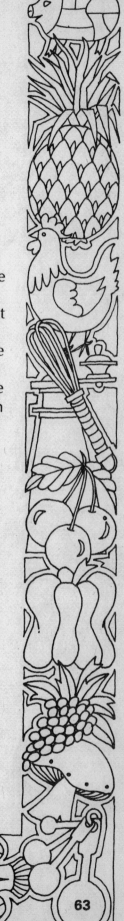

Fish & Seafoods

Fish Creole

2 lb (1 kg) fish fillets
2 tablespoons butter or margarine
2 onions, chopped
2 stalks celery, diced
1 green pepper, chopped
½ lb (250 g) tomatoes, sliced

½ bay leaf
2 tablespoons parsley, chopped
1 cup stale bread crumbs
1 teaspoon salt
7 whole black peppercorns
8 thin slices lemon

1. Heat butter or margarine in a frypan and saute the onions, celery and green pepper for five minutes. Add tomatoes, bay leaf and parsley and simmer for ten minutes. Stir in bread crumbs, salt and peppercorns.
2. Arrange half the fish in the bottom of a buttered casserole dish. Cover with part of the tomato mixture and 4 slices of lemon. Add the remaining fish and spread over the rest of the sauce and lemon slices.
3. Bake uncovered in a 350°F (180°C) oven for 30-40 minutes.

Serves 4-6.

Tuna Amandine

1 bunch asparagus spears, cooked	1 teaspoon salt
1 large can tuna fish, drained and flaked	¼ teaspoon pepper
½ cup (125 g) butter or margarine	⅛ teaspoon nutmeg
½ cup (60 g) blanched almonds, chopped	3 cups (750 ml) milk
5 tablespoons flour	2 tablespoons sherry
	paprika

1. Arrange asparagus spears on the bottom of a well-buttered baking dish. Cover with tuna fish.
2. Lightly brown the almonds in the butter or margarine. Blend in the flour, salt, pepper and nutmeg. Add the milk, stirring constantly. Cook until smooth and thick. Add the sherry.
3. Pour the sauce over the tuna, sprinkle with paprika and bake in a 350°F (180°C) oven for about 30 minutes.

Serves 6.

Shrimp Casserole

4 cups cooked shelled shrimp (about 2 lb (1 kg) with shells)	½ teaspoon pepper
2½ cups thinly sliced celery	1½ cups (187 g) dry bread crumbs
1 onion, finely chopped	½ cup (125 g) butter or margarine, melted
1 cup (250 ml) mayonnaise	lemon slices
2 teaspoons Worcestershire sauce	parsley
1 teaspoon salt	

1. Cut shrimp into bite-size pieces.
2. Mix the shrimp with the celery, onion, mayonnaise, Worcestershire sauce, salt and pepper. Spread mixture in a buttered casserole dish.
3. Combine bread crumbs and melted butter or margarine. Sprinkle over casserole.
4. Bake in a 350°F (180°C) oven for 30 minutes or until lightly browned. Serve garnished with lemon slices and parsley.

Serves 4-6.

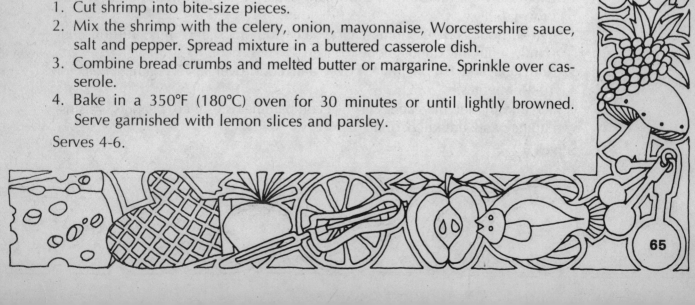

Quick Tuna Macaroni Casserole

1 cup (150 g) macaroni
1 can condensed cream of
   asparagus soup
⅔ cup (166 ml) evaporated
   milk

1 can tuna fish (large size)
½ red pepper, chopped
1 cup (125 g) grated cheddar
   cheese

1. Cook the macaroni in boiling salted water. Drain.
2. Combine asparagus soup and evaporated milk. Add macaroni, tuna, red pepper and ½ cup of cheese.
3. Pour into a greased casserole dish. Sprinkle with remaining cheese.
4. Bake in a 350°F (180°C) oven for 30 minutes.

Serves 4-6.

Tuna Curry

1 large can tuna fish packed
   in oil
1 medium onion, chopped
1 cooking apple, peeled,
   cored and chopped
6 tablespoons flour
curry powder to taste

1½ teaspoons salt
1 teaspoon sugar
¼ teaspoon ground ginger
1 cup (250 ml) chicken stock
2 cups (500 ml) milk
1 tablespoon lemon juice

1. Drain oil from tuna into a saucepan. Saute onion and apple until golden brown.
2. Mix in flour and seasonings. Gradually add stock and milk, stirring constantly, until thick and smooth.
3. Add tuna and lemon juice, cover and cook over a very gentle heat for 10-15 minutes.
4. Serve with hot rice and curry accompaniments: salted peanuts, raisins, chutney and grated coconut.

Serves 6.

Tuna and Vegetable Casserole

½ cup (125 g) butter or
margarine
1 onion, chopped
½ green pepper, chopped
3 tablespoons flour
1 teaspoon salt
¼ teaspoon pepper
¼ teaspoon paprika
⅛ teaspoon nutmeg

1½ cups (375 ml) milk
1 tablespoon lemon juice
1 large can tuna fish, packed
in oil
1 can corn niblets
1 cup crackers, crushed
¼ lb (125 g) cheddar cheese,
thinly sliced

1. Melt butter or margarine in the top of a double boiler. Add onion and green pepper and saute until onion is golden brown.
2. Gradually add flour, salt, pepper, paprika and nutmeg. Blend well. Place double boiler top over simmering water and add milk. Cook, stirring constantly, until mixture is thick and smooth. Add lemon juice and tuna oil and cook for ten minutes.
3. Flake the tuna and alternate in layers the tuna, cracker crumbs, corn, cheese and sauce.
4. Bake in a 450°F (230°C) oven for 15-10 minutes.

Serves 6.

Fish and Green Bean Casserole

4 cups green beans cut in
one-inch (2½ cm) pieces
boiling water
2 tablespoons butter or
margarine
salt and pepper

2 cups flaked cooked fish
½ cup (57 g) slivered almonds
2 tablespoons lemon juice
pinch of paprika
2 cups (500 ml) sour cream

1. Put green beans in a saucepan and add enough boiling water to cover. Cover and cook for about five minutes. Drain. Add butter or margarine and season to taste with salt and pepper.
2. Place beans in a casserole dish and cover with flaked fish and almonds. Sprinkle the fish with lemon juice and paprika and cover with sour cream.
3. Bake, covered, in a 350°F (180°C) oven for ½ hour.

Serves 6.

Tuna-Cheese Casserole

1 lb (500 g) macaroni	2 tablespoons flour
2 tablespoons butter or margarine	¼ lb (125 g) mild cheese, cut in pieces
1 cup (250 ml) milk	1 large can tuna fish

1. Cook macaroni in boiling salted water until tender. Drain well.
2. In the top of a double boiler melt butter or margarine. Blend in flour. Add milk, stirring constantly. Stir in cheese. Cook over simmering water until cheese is completely melted and sauce is thick.
3. Drain the tuna and place in the center of a shallow casserole dish.
4. Mix the macaroni with the cheese sauce and pour around the tuna.
5. Bake, covered, in a 375°F (190°C) oven for 20 minutes or until tuna is heated through.

Serves 6.

Deviled Fish

1 lb (500 g) fish fillets
1 clove garlic
1 medium onion, chopped
1 cup buttermilk (250 ml)
¼ lb (125 g) low-fat cottage
    cheese
curry powder to taste
salt and paprika
1½ tablespoons lemon juice

1. Place fish and garlic clove in the top of a double boiler and cover with boiling water. Cover and cook over boiling water until fish is tender (about 20-25 minutes.) Drain the fish and remove garlic. Flake the fish.
2. Combine the onion, buttermilk, cottage cheese and curry powder. Add to fish. Season to taste with salt and paprika and mix well. Place in a buttered casserole dish.
3. Bake in a 425°F (220°C) oven for 15 minutes. Sprinkle with lemon juice and serve immediately.

Serves 4.

Tuna and Egg Casserole

1 large can tuna fish, drained and flaked
1 cup (250 ml) cream
1½ teaspoons salt
¼ teaspoon pepper
½ onion, minced

3 hard-boiled eggs, chopped
2 teaspoons prepared mustard
½ cup (60 g) dry bread crumbs
2 tablespoons (40 g) butter or margarine, melted

1. Combine all ingredients except bread crumbs and butter.
2. Pour into a buttered casserole dish.
3. Mix the bread crumbs with the melted butter or margarine. Sprinkle over the tuna mixture.
4. Bake in a 375°F (190°C) oven until golden brown (about 30 minutes).

Serves 4.

Fish, Grapes and Mushroom Casserole

2 lb (1 kg) white fish fillets
2 cups (500 ml) milk
¼ cup (62.5 g) butter or margarine
¾ lb (375 g) mushrooms
2 cups seedless grapes, skinned

3 tablespoons (60 g) butter or margarine
6 tablespoons flour
1 teaspoon salt
¼ teaspoon pepper
½ cup buttered bread crumbs
¼ cup (30 g) Parmesan cheese, grated

1. Cover fish with milk and cook over a low heat for five minutes. Drain, reserving milk.
2. Melt ¼ cup butter or margarine. Add mushrooms and saute for five minutes. Add grapes, mix well and place in a casserole dish.
3. Place fish over mushrooms and grapes.
4. Melt the 3 tablespoons of butter or margarine. Blend in flour. Add reserved milk, stirring constantly. Cook, continuing to stir, over a low heat until thick and smooth. Add salt and pepper to taste. Pour sauce over fish. Sprinkle bread crumbs and cheese over top.
5. Bake in a 400°F (200°C) oven for about ½ hour.

Serves 6.

Fish Souffle

1 cup cooked fish, flaked	1 teaspoon salt
1 tablespoon butter or margarine	½ tablespoon minced onion
1 tablespoon flour	¼ teaspoon paprika
1 cup (250 ml) milk	pinch of tarragon, marjoram and nutmeg
2 eggs, separated	

1. Melt butter or margarine in a saucepan. Blend in flour. Gradually add milk, stirring constantly. Cook until smooth. Cool slightly.
2. Add beaten egg yolks to cooled white sauce. Add onion and seasonings. Stir in fish.
3. Beat egg whites until stiff. Fold into fish mixture. Pour into a casserole and bake in a 400°F (200°C) oven for 20 minutes.

Serves 4.

Shrimp Tetrazzini

½ lb (250 g) cooked peeled shrimp	1 teaspoon salt
2 cups cooked spaghetti	¼ teaspoon paprika
3 tablespoons butter or margarine (60 g)	¼ teaspoon pepper
3 tablespoons flour	½ cup (75 g) grated mild cheese
1½ cups (375 ml) milk	½ cup (55 g) bread crumbs
	1 avocado, sliced

1. In a shallow casserole dish arrange slices of peeled avocado. Place spaghetti on top of avocado.
2. Cut shrimp in halves and put on top of spaghetti.
3. Melt butter in a saucepan. Add flour and blend well. Gradually add milk, stirring constantly. Add salt, pepper and paprika and cook, stirring continuously, until the mixture is thick and smooth. Pour over the shrimp. Sprinkle with grated cheese and bread crumbs.
4. Bake, uncovered, in a 375°F (190°C) oven until heated through and browned.

Serves 6.

Salmon and Egg Casserole

4 tablespoons (80 g) butter or
  margarine
4 tablespoons chopped onion
1 stalk celery, chopped
4 tablespoons flour
2 cups (500 ml) milk
1 teaspoon salt
½ cup (75 g) grated cheddar
  cheese
pinch of pepper

1 teaspoon Worcestershire sauce
½ teaspoon dry mustard
6 hard-boiled eggs
¼ teaspoon salt
pinch of pepper
1 teaspoon prepared horseradish
  sauce
2 tablespoons lemon juice
1 lb (500 g) canned salmon

1. Melt butter or margarine in the top of a double boiler. Saute the onion
   and celery until tender.
2. Place over boiling water, add the flour and stir until well blended. Gradually add the milk and cook, stirring constantly, until the mixture is thick
   and smooth. Add the cheese, 1 teaspoon salt, pepper, Worcestershire
   sauce and mustard and stir until the cheese melts.
3. Cut eggs in half lengthwise. Remove yolks and reserve whites. Mash yolks
   and add ¼ teaspoon salt, pepper and horseradish. Moisten with ⅓ cup
   of cheese sauce. Refill whites with this mixture.
4. Arrange half of eggs in bottom of buttered casserole. Add lemon juice to
   salmon and arrange over eggs. Add remaining cheese sauce and top with
   remaining eggs.
5. Bake, covered, in a 350°F (180°C) oven for 30 minutes.

Serves 6.

Salmon and Cheese Casserole

1 cup (250 ml) milk, scalded
2 tablespoons (40 g) butter
  or margarine
2 cups (120 g) soft bread
  crumbs
1 cup (115 g) grated Parmesan
  cheese

1 lb (500 g) canned salmon,
  flaked
liquid from canned salmon
2 eggs, well-beaten

1. Melt butter or margarine in scalded milk. Add to bread crumbs and allow
   to stand for five minutes.
2. Add cheese, salmon and salmon liquid to the bread crumbs and mix well.
3. Add the egg, mix lightly and pour into a buttered casserole dish.
4. Bake in a 350°F (180°C) oven for 45 minutes.

Serves 4-6.

Creamed Noodles and Oysters

9 oz (280 g) noodles
boiling, salted water
¼ cup (62.5 g) butter or
    margarine
2 tablespoons flour
¾ cup (186 ml) milk

½ cup (125 ml) oyster liquid
½ teaspoon salt
¼ teaspoon pepper
2 dozen raw oysters
½ cup buttered bread crumbs

1. Cook the noodles in boiling salted water until tender. Drain and place in a casserole dish.
2. Melt butter or margarine in the top of a double boiler over boiling water. Add flour and blend well. Add the milk and oyster liquid and cook, stirring constantly, until mixture thickens. Season with salt and pepper. Chop oysters, if desired, and add to sauce. Cook for another five minutes. Pour over noodles. Sprinkle bread crumbs on top.
3. Bake in a 375°F (190°C) oven for 30 minutes.

Serves 4-6.

Oyster Casserole

4 tablespoons (80 g) butter or
    margarine
1 cup chopped celery
½ cup chopped onion
4 tablespoons flour
1 cup (250 ml) milk
½ cup (125 ml) oyster liquid

2 teaspoons salt
pinch of pepper
1 cup cooked peas
2 dozen oysters
3 medium potatoes, cooked
    and sliced

1. Melt butter or margarine in the top of a double boiler. Add celery and onion and cook until tender.
2. Place double boiler over boiling water. Add flour and blend well. Gradually add milk and oyster liquid and cook, stirring constantly, until the mixture thickens. Season with salt and pepper.
3. Put peas, oysters and potatoes in layers in a buttered casserole dish. Pour the sauce over the oysters and vegetables.
4. Bake, covered, in a 350°F (180°C) oven for 20 minutes. Uncover and cook for another 10 minutes.

Serves 4-6.

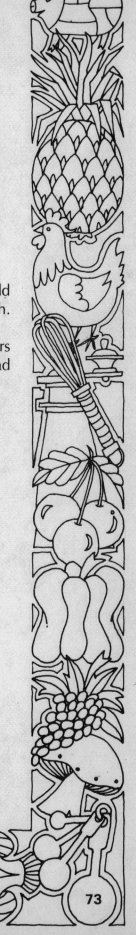

Corn and Oyster Casserole

2 tablespoons (40 g) butter
  or margarine
4 tablespoons flour
2 cups (500 ml) milk
1 teaspoon salt
⅛ teaspoon pepper
1½ cups corn niblets
2 eggs, slightly beaten
1½ cups oysters
salt and pepper
buttered bread crumbs

1. Melt butter or margarine in a saucepan. Add flour and blend well. Add milk and seasoning and cook, stirring constantly, until thick and smooth. Stir in corn and eggs.
2. Pour mixture into a buttered casserole dish. Arrange well-drained oysters on top. Sprinkle with salt and pepper and cover with buttered bread crumbs.
3. Bake in a 350°F (180°C) oven for ½ hour.

Serves 4.

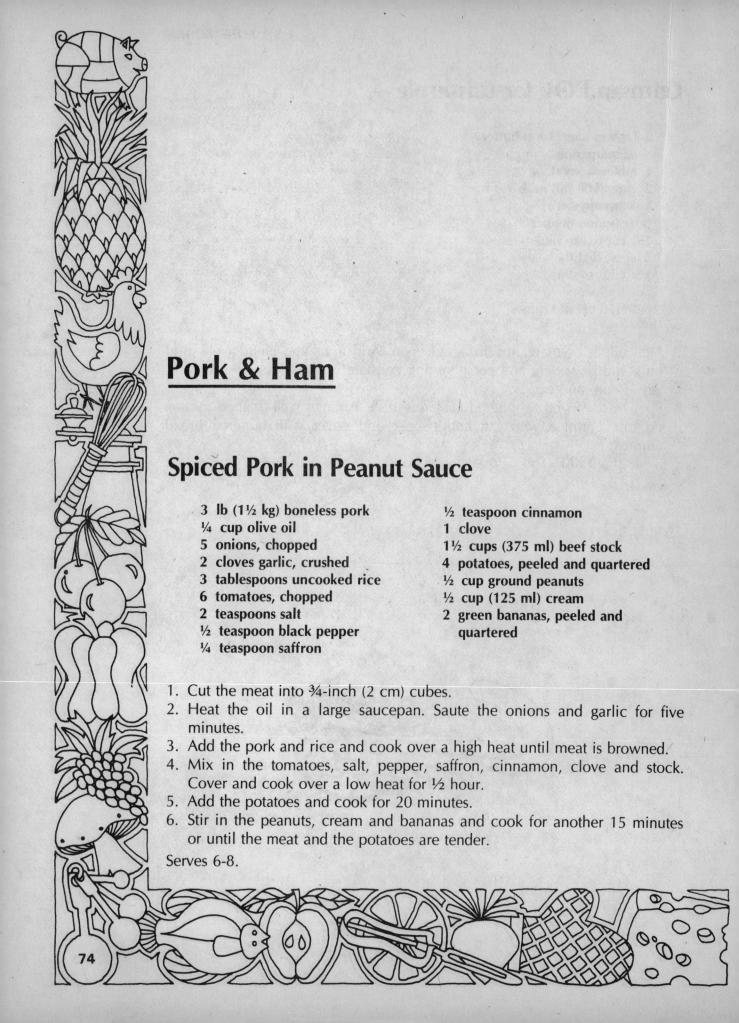

Pork & Ham

Spiced Pork in Peanut Sauce

3 lb (1½ kg) boneless pork
¼ cup olive oil
5 onions, chopped
2 cloves garlic, crushed
3 tablespoons uncooked rice
6 tomatoes, chopped
2 teaspoons salt
½ teaspoon black pepper
¼ teaspoon saffron

½ teaspoon cinnamon
1 clove
1½ cups (375 ml) beef stock
4 potatoes, peeled and quartered
½ cup ground peanuts
½ cup (125 ml) cream
2 green bananas, peeled and quartered

1. Cut the meat into ¾-inch (2 cm) cubes.
2. Heat the oil in a large saucepan. Saute the onions and garlic for five minutes.
3. Add the pork and rice and cook over a high heat until meat is browned.
4. Mix in the tomatoes, salt, pepper, saffron, cinnamon, clove and stock. Cover and cook over a low heat for ½ hour.
5. Add the potatoes and cook for 20 minutes.
6. Stir in the peanuts, cream and bananas and cook for another 15 minutes or until the meat and the potatoes are tender.

Serves 6-8.

Leftover Pork Casserole

5-7 slices stale bread	¼ teaspoon pepper
½ green pepper, chopped	1 teaspoon Worcestershire sauce
1 medium onion, chopped	leftover pork roast
½ cup (125 ml) tomato juice	1 cup (250 ml) leftover gravy
½ teaspoon salt	

1. Cut bread into small cubes and put in a mixing bowl. Mix in green pepper, onion, tomato juice, salt, pepper and Worcestershire sauce.
2. Put slices of leftover pork in a well-buttered casserole dish. Pour bread mixture over the top. Pour gravy over the bread mixture.
3. Bake in a 375°F (190°C) oven for 30 minutes.

Serves 4.

Pork Chops Stuffed with Prunes

½ lb (250 g) prunes	2 tablespoons oil
4 pork chops, one-inch	4 potatoes, thinly sliced
(2½ cm) thick	¼ cup (62.5 ml) hot water
juice of half lemon	
2 tablespoons brown sugar	

1. Soak the prunes in boiling water for 5-10 minutes. Drain and pit.
2. Bone the chops and make a pocket in each.
3. Chop the prunes, add the lemon juice, sugar and one tablespoon water. Simmer for two minutes.
4. Stuff the chops with the prune mixture. Heat the oil in a frypan and brown the chops on both sides.
5. Put into a casserole dish and cover with the potato slices. Pour the hot water over, cover and bake in a 350°F (180°C) oven for one hour. Remove the lid for the last 15 minutes to brown the potatoes.

Serves 4.

Pork and Prune Casserole

½ lb (250 g) prunes
juice and rind of one lemon
1½ lb (750 g) pork
4 tablespoons flour
salt and pepper
2 tablespoons (40 g) butter or
  margarine

1. In a saucepan, cover the prunes with cold water. Allow to soak for one hour, then cook over a low heat with the lemon rind for 15 minutes. Drain the prunes and reserve the liquid. Remove stones from the prunes.
2. Cut the pork into bite-size pieces and toss in the seasoned flour. Heat the butter or margarine in a frypan and brown the pork.
3. Put the prunes and pork in a casserole dish. Make a gravy with the remaining butter, flour and prune liquid. Pour over the pork. Stir in lemon juice.
4. Cover and cook in a 350°F (180°C) oven for one hour.

Serves 4.

Pork and Noodle Casserole

½ lb (250 g) uncooked noodles
¾ lb (375 g) ground pork
2 medium onions, chopped
2 cups diced celery
1 green pepper, chopped
salt and pepper
1 can (425 g) tomato soup
½ teaspoon Worcestershire sauce
½ cup grated cheese

1. Cook noodles in boiling salted water. Drain.
2. Brown meat in hot oil. Add onions, celery and green pepper. Cook until vegetables are tender. Season to taste with salt and pepper.
3. Alternate layers of meat and noodles in a well-buttered casserole.
4. Mix condensed soup with Worcestershire sauce and pour over meat and noodles. Sprinkle with cheese and bake in a 350°F (180°C) oven for 45 minutes.

Serves 4.

Spicy Baked Pork Chops

4 double pork chops
½ cup (80 g) raisins
2 teaspoons brown sugar
curry powder to taste
4 tablespoons minced onion
1 teaspoon salt
½ cup white wine

1. Cut a pocket in the center of each pork chop.
2. Combine raisins, sugar, curry powder and onion. Divide into four parts and insert stuffing in pork chops. Rub salt over pork chops.
3. Bake in a 450°F (230°C) oven until chops begin to brown — about 20 minutes. Spoon off excess fat. Reduce heat to 400°F (200°C). Pour over the wine and cook for another 15-20 minutes.

Serves 4.

Sausage Casserole

½ lb (250 g) bacon
2 lb (1 kg) pork sausages
1 lb (500 g) cooking apples,
    peeled, cored and sliced
1 lb (500 g) tomatoes
1 green pepper, chopped
¼ cup (62.5 ml) beef stock
salt and pepper

1. Wrap sausages with bacon and fry lightly. Place in a casserole dish.
2. Arrange the apples, tomatoes and pepper over the top of the sausages.
3. Add stock and seasoning. Cover and cook in a 400°F (200°C) oven for 45 minutes.

Serves 4-6.

Ground Pork and Beef Casserole

2 tablespoons butter or
  margarine
1 large onion, chopped
1 lb (500 g) ground beef
½ lb (250 g) ground pork
½ lb (250 g) noodles

1 can cream-style corn
1 can condensed tomato soup
½ cup (125 ml) tomato sauce
salt and pepper
grated cheese

1. Melt butter or margarine in a frypan. Saute onion until transparent. Add meat and cook, stirring constantly, until browned.
2. Cook noodles in boiling salted water until tender. Drain.
3. Mix noodles with the corn, tomato soup and tomato sauce. Combine with the meat mixture and season to taste with salt and pepper.
4. Put into a casserole dish and top with grated cheese. Bake in a 350°F (180°C) oven for one hour.

Serves 6-8.

Pork and Apple Casserole

6 pork chops
1 small onion, chopped
½ lb (250 g) noodles, cooked and
  drained
3 apples, cored and sliced
3 eggs
1 cup (250 ml) orange juice
salt and pepper

1. Brown pork chops on both sides in a frypan.
2. Remove pork chops and brown onions in drippings.
3. Put noodles, apples, onion and pan drippings in a well-buttered casserole dish.
4. Beat eggs with orange juice. Pour mixture over noodles. Top with browned pork chops. Sprinkle meat with salt and pepper.
5. Cover and bake in a 350°F (180°C) for 45 minutes.

Serves 6.

Ham Hotpot

1 lb (500 g) ham, cut
  into cubes
½ lb (250 g) peas
2 onions, chopped
½ lb (250 g) potatoes, sliced

5 peppercorns
¼ teaspoon mixed herbs
⅔ cup (166 ml) water
salt and pepper

1. Arrange ham and vegetables in layers in a greased casserole dish. Season with salt, pepper and mixed herbs between layers.
2. End with a layer of potatoes. Add the peppercorns and water.
3. Cover and cook in a 350°F (180°C) for one hour. Remove the top of the dish to allow potatoes to brown for the last fifteen minutes of cooking.

Serves 4.

Apple and Pork Hotpot

8 loin pork chops
1 lb (500 g) cooking apples,
  sliced
2 onions, chopped
4 tablespoons oil

1 lb (500 g) tomatoes, peeled
  and quartered
1 lb (500 g) potatoes, peeled
  and diced
salt and pepper

1. Saute the apples and onions in the oil until they are golden brown.
2. Put the chops in a casserole dish and cover with the apples, onions, tomatoes and potatoes.
3. Add seasoning and half cover with water.
4. Cover and cook in a 350°F (180°C) oven for 1½-2 hours.

Serves 6-8.

Ham Steaks with Cheese

½ cup (125 ml) cream
½ lb (250 g) sharp cheese, diced
2 tablespoons lemon juice
½ teaspoon Worcestershire sauce
1 teaspoon prepared mustard
pinch cayenne pepper
4-6 ham steaks

1. Heat cream in the top of a double boiler over hot water. Add cheese, lemon juice, Worcestershire sauce, mustard and pepper. Cook, stirring constantly, until cheese melts and sauce is smooth.
2. Lightly saute ham on both sides. Place in casserole dish and pour cheese sauce over the steaks.
3. Bake in a 350°F (180°C) oven for about 30 minutes.

Serves 4-6.

Turkey-Ham Casserole

1 cup chopped onion
1 cup diced green pepper
½ cup (125 g) butter or margarine
¾ cup, sliced black olives
½ teaspoon salt
1 teaspoon oregano
1½ cups cooked turkey, diced

1½ cups cooked ham, diced
2½ cups cooked noodles
2 cups pureed apples
2 tablespoons butter
   or margarine, melted
paprika

1. Saute onion and green pepper in butter or margarine until lightly browned. Add olives, salt and oregano and heat thoroughly.
2. Place ½ cup noodles in the bottom of a well-buttered casserole dish.
3. Mix turkey and ham and place with the onion, pepper and olive mixture on top of noodles.
4. Spoon apple puree over the top.
5. Toss remaining noodles in the two tablespoons of butter or margarine. Place on top of apple puree. Sprinkle with paprika. Bake in a 375°F (190°C) oven for about 30 minutes.

Serves 6-8.

Pork and Turnip Casserole

5 lb (2½ kg) loin of pork
2 teaspoons salt
½ teaspoon black pepper
¼ teaspoon crushed bay leaf
¼ teaspoon thyme
1 clove garlic, crushed
2 tablespoons vegetable oil

2 carrots, sliced
3 white onions, quartered
4 potatoes, peeled and quartered
4 turnips, peeled and quartered
   lengthwise
½ cup (125 ml) dry vermouth

1. Rub the pork with a mixture of the salt, pepper, bay leaf, thyme and garlic. Let stand for two hours at room temperature.
2. Heat the oil in a flame-proof casserole. Brown the pork in it. Pour off all but two tablespoons of fat and turn the meat fat side up.
3. Add the carrots and cook in a 325°F (160°C) oven for 1½ hours, basting frequently.
4. Pour boiling water over the onions, potatoes and turnips. Let stand for ten minutes. Drain.
5. Add the vegetables to the pork with the vermouth. Cover and bake for another hour, basting frequently.

Serves 6-8.

Creole Pork Casserole

6 pork chops, cut
   1½ inches (4 cm) thick
3½ teaspoons salt
1 teaspoon pepper
2 tablespoons oil
3 potatoes, thinly sliced
2 onions, thinly sliced

1 green pepper, sliced
1 clove garlic, crushed
1 lb (500 g) tomatoes, chopped
½ teaspoon thyme
1 bay leaf
4 tablespoons chopped parsley

1. Rub the pork chops with 2 teaspoons salt and ½ teaspoon pepper.
2. Coat the bottom of a casserole dish with the oil.
3. Arrange the potatoes on the bottom. Season with a little salt. Place the chops over them. Spread the chops with the onions, green pepper, garlic, tomatoes, thyme, bay leaf, parsley and remaining salt and pepper.
4. Cover and bake in a 375°F (190°C) oven for about 1½ hours or until chops are tender. Remove the bay leaf.

Serves 6.

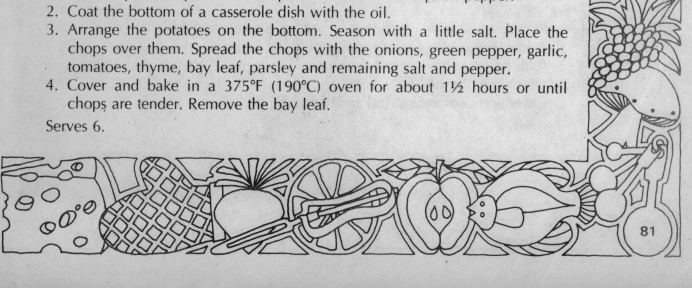

Braised Pork with Beans

3 cups (600 g) dried beans	½ cup olive oil
4 teaspoons salt	4 onions, chopped
2 lb (1 kg) boneless pork, cut into one-inch (2½ cm) cubes	2 cloves garlic, crushed
	¼ cup chopped onion
½ teaspoon black pepper	½ cup (60 g) grated cheddar cheese
2 cups (500 ml) boiling water	

1. Wash the beans. Cover with water and bring to a boil. Let soak for one hour. Drain. Add fresh water to cover and bring to boil. Cook over a low heat for two hours or until tender. After one hour of cooking, add two teaspoons of salt. Drain if any liquid remains.
2. Brown the pork in a large saucepan. Season with the remaining salt and pepper. Add the boiling water and cook over a low heat for 30 minutes.
3. Heat the oil in a large saucepan. Saute the four onions for ten minutes. Add the undrained pork, the garlic, and beans.
4. Cover and cook over low heat for ½ hour. Sprinkle with the onions and grated cheese.

Serves 4-6.

Hungarian Pork Stew

4 lb (2 kg) pork, cut into 1½-inch (4 cm) cubes	½ teaspoon black pepper
2 tablespoons (40 g) butter or margarine	2 cloves garlic, crushed
	2 green peppers, chopped
4 onions, sliced	1 tablespoon tomato paste
2 tablespoons paprika	½ teaspoon basil
2 teaspoons salt	1 cup (250 ml) boiling water

1. Melt the butter or margarine in a large saucepan. Saute the onions until golden brown. Remove from heat and stir in the paprika, salt and pepper.
2. Add the meat, garlic, green peppers, lemon juice, tomato paste, basil and one cup of the boiling water.
3. Cover and cook over a low heat for three hours.

Serves 8.

Pork and Tomato Casserole

1 lb (500 g) ground pork
2 onions, chopped
2 tablespoons oil
1½ cups cooked macaroni
½ lb (250 g) tomatoes, chopped
½ cup (125 ml) tomato juice
1 cup (125 g) grated cheese
½ cup bread crumbs

1. Heat oil in a frypan and brown onions and pork, stirring constantly. Drain off excess fat.
2. Add macaroni, tomatoes, tomato juice, salt and ½ cup cheese.
3. Put into a casserole dish. Sprinkle with remaining cheese and bread crumbs.
4. Bake in a 350°F (180°C) oven for 45 minutes.

Serves 4.

Apple and Ham Casserole

3 cooking apples
3 medium sweet potatoes, cooked
  and sliced
1 teaspoon dry mustard
2 cups diced ham
¼ cup (62.5 ml) water or
  apple juice
4 tablespoons brown sugar

1. Peel, core and slice the apples in rounds.
2. Arrange apple rounds, sliced sweet potatoes and ham in layers in a greased casserole dish, ending with apple rounds. Sprinkle each layer with mustard.
3. Add water or apple juice, cover and bake for 45-50 minutes in a 350°F (180°C) oven. Remove cover, sprinkle with brown sugar and bake for another ten minutes.

Serves 4-6.

Ham and Egg Casserole

7 tablespoons (140 g) butter or margarine	pinch of pepper
¼ cup flour	6 hard-boiled eggs, sliced
2 cups (500 ml) milk	½ lb (250 g) cooked cubed ham
½ teaspoon salt	¼ lb (125 g) mushrooms
	1 cup crushed cornflakes

1. Melt 4 tablespoons of the butter or margarine in the top of a double boiler. Stir in the flour. Gradually add the milk and cook, stirring constantly, until the mixture thickens. Season with salt and pepper.
2. Arrange alternate layers of hard-boiled eggs, ham and mushrooms in a buttered casserole dish.
3. Pour on the white sauce.
4. Melt the remaining butter or margarine and mix with the cornflakes. Sprinkle over the top of the casserole.
5. Bake in a 350°F (180°C) for about 30 minutes.

Serves 6.

Country Ham and Potatoes

4 ham steaks
1 tablespoon prepared mustard
bread crumbs
2 large potatoes, sliced
2 large onions, sliced
1 cup (250 ml) milk, heated
salt and pepper

1. Spread the ham steaks with prepared mustard and dip in bread crumbs.
2. Arrange layers of potatoes, onions and steaks in a buttered casserole dish, seasoning each layer with salt and pepper and sprinkling with crumbs. Reserve four slices of potatoes for the top.
3. Pour hot milk over filled casserole and then arrange the four slices of potatoes on the top. Sprinkle with bread crumbs.
4. Bake in a 350°F (180°C) oven for one hour or until potatoes are cooked and the liquid is almost absorbed.

Serves 4.

Ground Pork Stew

½ cup olive oil
6 onions, chopped
2 lb (1 kg) ground pork
2 cloves garlic, crushed
4 tomatoes, chopped
2 cans chick peas, drained
3½ teaspoons salt
¼ teaspoon chili powder

2 cups (420 g) uncooked rice
1 green pepper, chopped
1 lb can tomatoes
2 cups (500 ml) boiling water
½ teaspoon pepper
½ teaspoon oregano
½ cup (83 g) seedless raisins
½ cup (60 g) slivered almonds

1. Heat half the oil in a large saucepan. Brown half the onion in it.
2. Mix in the pork and half the garlic until browned.
3. Add the fresh tomatoes, chick peas, 1½ teaspoons salt and the chili powder. Cover and cook over a low heat for 45 minutes.
4. Heat the remaining oil in a saucepan. Saute the rice, green pepper and remaining onions until browned.
5. Mix in the canned tomatoes, boiling water, pepper, oregano and the remaining garlic and salt. Cover and cook over a low heat for 25 minutes. Mix in the raisins and almonds.
6. Combine the rice mixture with the pork mixture.

Serves 6-8.

Pork and Bean Casserole

6 pork chops, cut ¾ inch
  (2 cm) thick
1½ teaspoons pepper
½ teaspoon pepper
1 tablespoon oil

2 onions, chopped
1 clove garlic, crushed
½ teaspoon dry mustard
½ cup (125 ml) chili sauce
3 cans kidney beans, drained

1. Trim the fat off the chops. Season with the salt and pepper.
2. Heat the oil in a frypan. Add the chops and cook over a low heat until browned on both sides. Remove the chops.
3. Pour off all but two tablespoons fat. In the remaining fat, saute the onions and garlic for five minutes. Stir in the mustard, chili sauce and beans. Season to taste with salt and pepper.
4. Arrange the chops on top. Cover and bake in a 350°F (180°C) oven for 45 minutes.

Serves 6.

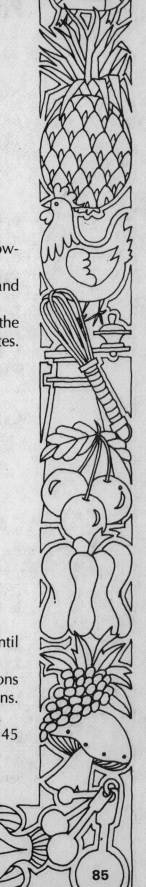

Pork with Orange Casserole

6 pork chops, cut
  one inch (2½ cm) thick
2 teaspoons salt
¼ teaspoon pepper
2 lb (1 kg) sweet potatoes,
  cooked and peeled
½ cup firmly packed
  brown sugar

¼ cup (62.5 g) butter or
  margarine, melted
3 tablespoons rum
2 oranges, peeled and diced
½ cup chopped nuts

1. Season the chops with 1½ teaspoons salt and the pepper. Brown on both sides in a frypan. Drain and arrange in a casserole dish.
2. Mash the sweet potatoes and mix in ¼ cup of brown sugar, half the butter, the remaining salt and the rum. Fold in the oranges and spread over the chops.
3. Mix together the nuts and the remaining brown sugar and butter. Sprinkle over the top.
4. Bake in a 375°F (190°C) oven for 30 minutes.

Serves 6.

Ground Pork and Green Beans

1½ lb (750 g) green beans, cut
  crosswise in ¼-inch (½ cm)
  slices
3 tablespoons vegetable oil
2 lb (1 kg) ground pork
1 clove garlic, crushed
1 teaspoon salt

2 tablespoons soy sauce
1½ cups (375 ml) water
¼ lb (125 g) bean sprouts
2 teaspoons cornstarch
1 cup shredded lettuce
½ onion, sliced

1. Heat the oil in a saucepan. Add the pork and garlic and cook over a medium heat, stirring constantly, until browned.
2. Add the salt, soy sauce and cook for one minute.
3. Add one cup water and bring to a boil. Stir in the green beans and bean sprouts. Cook one minute. Cover and cook for two minutes.
4. Mix the cornstarch with the remaining water and stir into the pork mixture until thickened.
5. Spread lettuce in a hot serving dish. Pour meat mixture over it. Sprinkle with onions.

Serves 4-6.

Pork and Bean Sprouts

2 lb (1 kg) boneless pork
4 tablespoons oil
2 onions, sliced
1½ cups (375 ml) chicken stock
2 cups cooked rice
1 stalk celery, thinly sliced
¼ lb (125 g) mushrooms, sliced

½ lb (250 g) bean sprouts
1 tablespoon cornstarch
1 tablespoon salt
¼ teaspoon pepper
1 teaspoon brown sugar
3 tablespoons soy sauce
2 tablespoons dry sherry

1. Cut the pork into very thin strips. Heat the oil in a large frypan. Saute the pork in it for 15 minutes.
2. Add the onions and cook for three minutes.
3. Mix in the chicken stock, rice, celery, mushrooms and bean sprouts. Bring to a boil and cook over a low heat for five minutes.
4. Blend together the cornstarch, salt, pepper, sugar, soy sauce and sherry. Stir into the frypan until thickened.

Serves 4-6.

Baked Pork and Sauerkraut

2 tablespoons oil
2 onions, sliced
6 pork chops, cut one-inch
   (2½ cm) thick
2 teaspoons salt
½ teaspoon black pepper
1 lb (500 g) sauerkraut
2 cups pureed apricots
¼ teaspoon caraway seeds

1. Heat the oil in a frypan. Saute the onion for five minutes. Remove the onions.
2. In the oil remaining brown the chops. Season with salt and pepper.
3. Rinse the sauerkraut under cold running water. Drain well. Mix with the apricots, caraway seeds and sauteed onions.
4. Spread sauerkraut mixture in a greased casserole dish. Arrange chops over the mixture.
5. Cover and bake in a 350°F (180°C) oven for 1¼ hours, removing cover for the last 15 minutes.

Serves 6.

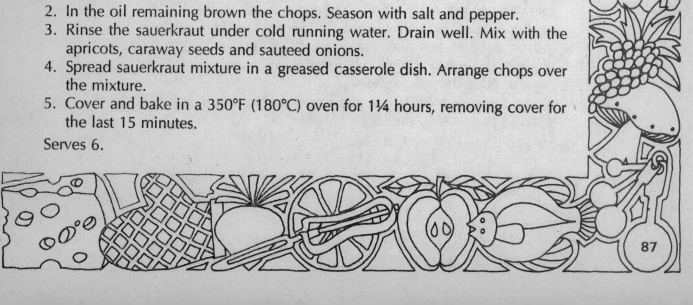

Potatoes with Ham Casserole

¼ cup (62.5 g) sour cream
3 tablespoons cream
1 teaspoon salt
2½ tablespoons (50 g) butter
   or margarine
1 lb (500 g) cooked potatoes,
   thinly sliced

4 hard-boiled eggs
½ lb (250 g) chopped ham
1¼ cups fresh bread crumbs
2½ tablespoons (50 g) butter
   or margarine, melted

1. Blend together the sour cream, cream and salt.
2. In a well-buttered casserole dish, arrange one-third of the potatoes with a layer of sliced egg on top. Pour over one-third of the cream mixture. Add another third of the potatoes, sprinkle with two-thirds of the chopped ham. Pour remaining cream mixture over. Top with the rest of the potatoes.
3. Mix the remaining ham with the bread crumbs and melted butter or margarine. Sprinkle over the top layer of potatoes.
4. Bake in a 350°F (180°C) oven for 30 minutes.

Serves 4.

Carolina Ham Casserole

4 tablespoons (80 g) butter or
   margarine
4 tablespoons flour
2 cups (500 ml) milk
1 teaspoon salt
½ teaspoon black pepper

1 green pepper, chopped
1 lb (500 g) ham, diced
2 cups cooked rice
4 apples, peeled and thinly
   sliced
½ cup brown sugar

1. Melt the butter or margarine in a saucepan. Stir in the flour until smooth. Slowly add the milk, stirring constantly until thick. Add the salt, pepper and green pepper and cook over a low heat for five minutes.
2. Mix in the ham and rice. Add more salt if desired.
3. Pour mixture into a well-buttered casserole and arrange the apple slices on top. Sprinkle with brown sugar.
4. Place the casserole in a shallow pan of hot water and bake in a 350°F (180°C) oven for 30 minutes.

Serves 4.

Others

Turkey Tetrazzini

4 lb (2 kg) cooked diced turkey
½ cup (125 g) butter or
  margarine
½ cup flour
3 cups (750 ml) chicken stock
2 cups (500 ml) milk
1 cup (250 ml) cream
salt and pepper
1 lb (500 g) spaghetti
½ lb (250 g) mushrooms, sliced
1 cup (125 g) dry bread crumbs
1 cup (115 g) grated Parmesan
  cheese

1. Melt butter or margarine in a saucepan. Stir in flour. Add chicken stock and milk, stirring constantly. Cook until mixture is thick and smooth. Stir in cream and season to taste with salt and pepper.
2. Cook spaghetti in boiling salted water until tender. Drain and put in a greased casserole dish.
3. Put meat over the spaghetti. Add mushrooms and pour sauce over all.
4. Mix bread crumbs with cheese and sprinkle on top of the casserole.
5. Bake in a 425°F (220°C) oven for 25-30 minutes.

Serves 10.

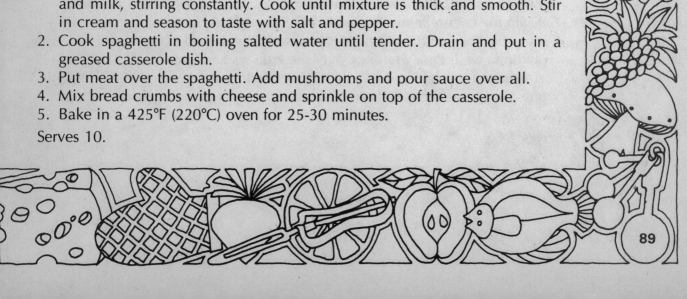

Baked Eggs in Eggplant

1 medium eggplant	chili powder to taste
1 onion, chopped	1 teaspoon salt
1 green pepper, chopped	¼ teaspoon pepper
2 tablespoons oil	6 eggs
2 tomatoes, cut in small pieces	buttered bread crumbs

1. Peel the eggplant and cut into one-inch (2½ cm) cubes. Boil for five minutes. Drain.
2. Heat oil and saute the onion and green pepper until onion is transparent. Add the tomatoes, eggplant and seasoning and simmer for 10 minutes.
3. Pour the vegetable mixture into a well-greased casserole dish. Gently break the eggs into it and sprinkle some buttered bread crumbs on top.
4. Bake in a 400°F (200°C) oven for 10 minutes or until the eggs are set.

Serves 6.

Kidney Casserole

1½ lb (750 g) kidneys	salt and pepper
2 medium onions, chopped	⅔ cup (166 ml) beef stock
2 tablespoons oil	boiled rice
6 slices bacon	chopped parsley
2 tablespoons flour	

1. Halve and skin the kidneys. Remove the cores and soak in cold salted water for five minutes.
2. Saute the onions in the oil until golden brown. Put into a casserole dish and cover with the drained kidneys.
3. Saute the bacon lightly, break into pieces and add to the kidneys.
4. Mix the flour with salt and pepper, sprinkle over the bacon and kidneys and mix well. Pour the stock over the kidneys and bacon.
5. Cover and cook in a 350°F (180°C) oven for about half an hour or until the kidneys are tender. Serve with fluffy white rice and garnish with parsley.

Serves 4-6.

Bologna Jamboree

½ lb (250 g) bologna, diced
3 cups hot cooked noodles
1 teaspoon salt
¼ teaspoon pepper
1 cup (250 ml) cream
½ cup bread crumbs
1 tablespoon butter or
   margarine (20 g)

1. Place diced bologna and cooked noodles in alternate layers in a casserole dish. Season with salt and pepper.
2. Pour on cream and sprinkle bread crumbs over the top. Dot with butter or margarine.
3. Heat in a 400°F (200°C) oven for about ½ hour.

Serves 4.

Vegetable-Frankfurter Casserole

8 frankfurters
1 large onion, sliced
1 large green pepper, sliced
4 medium tomatoes, sliced
1 can corn niblets
1½ teaspoons salt
¼ teaspoon pepper

1. In a casserole arrange layer of sliced onion, sliced pepper, sliced tomatoes and corn, seasoning with salt and pepper.
2. Top with frankfurters cut in half lengthwise.
3. Bake in a 375°F (190°C) oven for 45 minutes.

Serves 4.

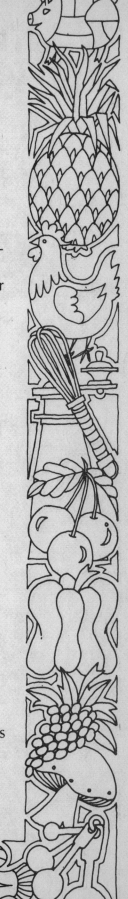

Rabbit Hotpot

1 lb (500 g) rabbit
½ lb (250 g) carrots, sliced
1 lb (500 g) potatoes, quartered
1 package onion soup mix

1. Joint the rabbit and wash well. Blanch by putting into a saucepan, covering with water and bringing it to a boil. Remove the rabbit from the saucepan and place in a casserole dish.
2. Put carrots and potatoes over the rabbit.
3. Mix the soup with 2½ cups (625 ml) hot water and pour over the vegetables and rabbit.
4. Cover and cook in a 350°F (180°C) oven for two hours.

Serves 4.

Tripe Stew

1 lb (500 g) tripe
1½ tablespoons oil
1 onion, chopped
4 tablespoons flour
1¾ cups (436 ml) chicken stock
1 carrot, sliced
1 tablespoon tomato sauce
salt to taste
bouquet garni
1 bay leaf
3 tablespoons vinegar

1. Wash the tripe and cut into bite-size pieces.
2. Heat the oil and lightly saute the onion. Stir in the flour and slowly add the chicken stock, stirring constantly.
3. Bring to a boil, stirring continuously and add the carrot, tomato sauce, salt, bouquet garni and bay leaf.
4. Mix in the tripe and vinegar, cover and simmer gently for about two hours. Remove the bouquet garni and bay leaf after one hour.

Serves 4.

Oxtail Hotpot

1 oxtail, jointed
seasoned flour
2 tablespoons oil
3 onions, sliced
½ lb (250 g) carrots, chopped
4 tomatoes, chopped
3 potatoes, diced
salt and pepper
beef stock

1. Toss the oxtail in the seasoned flour and brown in hot oil. Put in a casserole dish.
2. Saute the onions in the oil (adding more if necessary) until golden brown.
3. Add the onions to meat with the other vegetables. Season to taste with salt and pepper. Half cover the meat and vegetables with beef stock. Cover and cook in a 300°F (150°C) oven for four hours.

Serves 4.

Spaghetti Casserole

½ lb (250 g) spaghetti
4 hard-boiled eggs, sliced
3 tomatoes, sliced
½ lb (250 g) ham, chopped
2 tablespoons butter or margarine
4 tablespoons flour
2 cups (500 ml) milk
1 cup (115 g) grated Parmesan
    cheese
salt and pepper

1. Cook the spaghetti in boiling salted water until tender. Drain well.
2. Put alternate layers of spaghetti, tomato, egg and ham in a casserole dish.
3. Make a white sauce of the butter or margarine, flour, milk and half the cheese. Season to taste with salt and pepper. Pour the sauce over the spaghetti and sprinkle the other half of the cheese on top.
4. Bake in a 350°F (180°C) oven for about ½ hour or until the top is browned.

Serves 4-6.

Scalloped Potatoes and Frankfurter Casserole

3 potatoes, thinly sliced
1 medium onion, thinly sliced
salt and pepper
1 teaspoon garlic salt
4 tablespoons flour
8 frankfurters
1 tablespoon butter or margarine
2 cups (500 ml) milk

1. Place half of the potatoes and onion in a casserole dish. Sprinkle with salt, pepper and half the garlic salt and half the flour.
2. Cut frankfurters into one-inch (2½ cm) pieces and place on top of potatoes. Cover with remaining potatoes. Sprinkle with salt, pepper and the remaining garlic salt and flour.
3. Dot with butter or margarine and pour the milk over the top.
4. Cover and bake in a 350°F (180°C) oven for 45 minutes. Uncover and bake for another 20 minutes or until potatoes are tender.

Serves 4.

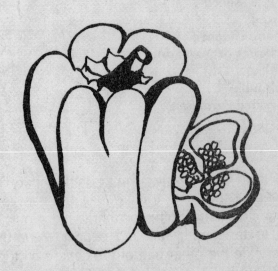

Index

Apple and ham casserole 83
Apple and pork hotpot 79

Bacon and lamb casserole 58
Barcelona beef stew 23
Baked eggs in eggplant 90
Baked pork and sauerkraut 87
Beans and beef 11
Beef and beer casserole 24
Beef and potato casserole 9
Beef and rice stew in sour cream sauce 37
Beef and sauerkraut 21
Beef in sesame seed sauce 27
Beef Bourguignon 30
Beef in lemon sauce 36
Beef stew in black sauce 37
Beef stew in horseradish sauce 29
Beef stew with dumplings 40
Beef stew Toulouse 10
Beef stroganoff 14
Beef, sweet potato and pineapple casserole 39
Beef with eggplant casserole 18
Bologna Jamboree 91
Braised beef in beer 28
Braised beef with ham 38
Braised chicken with peas 49
Braised lamb in sour cream 57
Braised liver casserole 16
Braised pork with beans 82
Braised veal cutlets 32
Brunswick stew 47
Bulgarian casserole 31

Carolina ham casserole 88
Casseroled leg of veal 33
Chicken and beef casserole 39
Chicken and cabbage stew 46
Chicken curry 43
Chicken in cream 48
Chicken in sour cream sauce 48
Chicken in whisky sauce 49

Chicken paprika 42
Chicken pie 45
Chicken-rice casserole 43
Chicken-rice curry 46
Chicken vermouth with wine 44
Chicken with pineapple 44
Chicken with prunes 47
Chili con carne 15
Corn and oyster casserole 73
Country ham and potatoes 84
Creamed noodles and oysters 72
Creole pork casserole 81
Curried lamb 52
Curried lamb stew 56

Deviled fish 68

Family meat pie 16
Fish and green bean casserole 67
Fish creole 64
Fish, grapes and mushroom casserole 69
Fish souffle 70
Fruity hotpot 14

Ground beef and celery casserole 12
Ground beef and macaroni casserole 11
Ground lamb curry 62
Ground pork and beef casserole 78
Ground pork and green beans 86
Ground pork stew 85

Ham and egg casserole 84
Ham hotpot 79
Ham steaks with cheese 80
Hotpot 25
Hungarian beef goulash 20
Hungarian pork stew 82

Kidney casserole 90

Lamb and barley stew 62

Lamb and bean stew 61
Lamb and celery stew 53
Lamb and rice a la Greque 61
Lamb curry 53
Lamb hotpot 60
Lamb paprika 51
Lamb pulao 58
Lamb shanks with rice 60
Lamb stew with sour cream 55
Lamb-vegetable casserole 59
Lamb with peaches 57
Lancashire casserole 56
Leftover beef casserole 15
Leftover beef stew 17
Leftover pork casserole 75
Liver and bacon pie 22
Liver in wine 19

Marinated pot roast 35
Meal-in-a-dish chicken casserole 42

North country casserole 52

Old fashioned beef stew 31
Oriental chicken with rice 41
Oxtail hotpot 93
Oyster casserole 72

Pepper pot stew 13
Persian lamb stew 54
Pilaf with lamb patties 55
Pineapple lamb casserole 51
Pork and apple casserole 78
Pork and bean casserole 85
Pork and bean sprouts 87
Pork and noodle casserole 76
Pork and prune casserole 76
Pork and tomato casserole 83
Pork and turnip casserole 81
Pork chops stuffed with prunes 75
Pork with orange casserole 86
Potato-beef pie 18
Potatoes with ham casserole 88
Pot roast with prunes and sweet potatoes 28
Pot roast, Swedish style 36
Provence casserole 63

Quick tuna macaroni casserole 66

Rabbit hotpot 92
Ragout of beef 19
Red cabbage and beef stew 17
Rich veal stew 32
Roast lamb casserole 54
Rosemary beef casserole 20
Rump steak and olive casserole 13

Salmon and cheese casserole 71
Salmon and egg casserole 71

Sausage casserole 77
Sausage macaroni casserole 30
Scalloped potatoes and frankfurter casserole 94
Shin of beef and vegetable casserole 12
Shrimp casserole 65
Shrimp tetrazzini 70
Spaghetti casserole 93
Special beef stew 27
Special veal casserole 34
Spiced pork in peanut sauce 74
Spicy baked pork chops 77
Spicy lamb stew with dumplings 50
Spicy steak casserole 25
Steak and kidney hotpot 22
Swedish lamb stew 59
Swedish sailors stew 24
Sweet and sour beef 21
Sweet potato chicken pie 45

Tomato and beef casserole 29
Tuna Amandine 65
Tuna and egg casserole 69
Tuna and vegetable casserole 67
Tuna-cheese casserole 68
Tuna curry 66
Tripe stew 92
Turkey-ham casserole 80
Turkey tetrazzini 89

Veal and noodle supreme 26
Veal-beef-pork casserole 38
Veal hotpot 34
Veal shank stew 33
Vegetable-frankfurter casserole 91
Vegetable meat loaf 26

West Indian beef stew 10

8000-4-S65